BEGINNING BACKGAMMON

Tim Holland   **BEGINNING**

BACKGAMMON

David McKay, *New York*

Beginning Backgammon

COPYRIGHT © 1973 BY Tim Holland

All rights reserved, including the right to reproduce
this book, or parts thereof, in any form, except for
the inclusion of brief quotations in a review.

Library of Congress Catalog Card Number: 73-84051

MANUFACTURED IN THE UNITED STATES OF AMERICA

ISBN: 0-679-50405-2 (Cloth)

ISBN: 0-679-73049-1 (Paper)

Designed by Bob Antler

10 9 8 7 6 5 4

Contents

To
Lona, my wife

Foreword

WELCOME TO BACKGAMMON—an age-old game perfectly suited to modern times. It is the oldest game in recorded history and has often been called the aristocrat of popular games. Though only in the last decade has backgammon caught on in the United States, like good wines and incense it has been popular elsewhere for centuries.

Essentially a running and blocking contest based on mathematical probabilities, each player simultaneously protects his own men while trying to advance them toward home and offensively attacks his opponent's men in order to retard their progress. The game is quick, calculating, decisive, and yet unpredictable until the very end. As luck will have it (and the luck of the toss is a definite uncontrollable factor), it is also—at times—frustrating and exasperating, exhilarating and rewarding.

One board, a pair of dice, thirty men, and a doubling cube—these are the raw material for billions of possibilities. Every contest is a unique combination of skill and chance. There probably never have been two games played exactly the same way in the long, long history of backgammon.

Excavated relics and extant literary references indicate the game's popularity among the ancient aristocracies of Greece, Rome, Persia, and the Far East as far back as Biblical times. From way back when, backgammon players have been in good, if occasionally notorious, company. Plato mentioned the game and its popularity among Greek high society. Later literary allusions indicate the Roman ruling classes also considered the game extremely fashionable and pleasurable. The emperor Claudius even wrote a book on the subject, perhaps to clarify the nobility of the game, for his predecessor Caligula was known as a cheat.

The Romans, however they played, called the game *tabula*, most likely after the table or board on which it was played. When the Romans invaded Britain, they imported *tabula* with them. The English anglicized the name of the game to "tables" and kept it as a popular aristocratic pastime throughout the Middle Ages.

Elsewhere, various forms of the game entranced the upper classes. *Grand trictrac*, probably so-called in imitation of the sound of the rattle of the dice, was *très chic* in French high society in the seventeenth and eighteenth centuries. Several allegorical engravings dating to that period depict European nobility playing trictrac in apparent satire of playing power politics. Without mincing words, the Italians played *tavole reale* and the Spanish *tablas reales*, both translating to "royal tables."

By the early seventeenth century in England, the game was refined into an approximation of today's game, except for the addition of the doubling cube, which was added in 1925. According to the *Oxford Universal Dictionary*, the name backgammon was coined around 1645 although the more popular term "tables" persisted for at least a few decades more. Most likely *backgammon* combines the Middle English word *baec*, meaning "back," and *gamen*, meaning "game." Word-lovers, however, may take note that in Welsh the words *bach* and *cammaun* suitably translate to "small battle."

Edmond Hoyle—who else?—codified the rules of proper play in a treatise in 1743. And, indeed, references in English history indicate that several kings, dukes, and members of the landed gentry considered backgammon *the* proper game for English gentlemen.

By the mid-nineteenth century, Americans, perhaps in emulation of English manners, began to play backgammon in increasing numbers on their own estates and in exclusive clubs and resorts. About that time, one clever observer of the society around him noted that democracy was too new to have yet been able to organize its pleasures. Local politics aside, certain sports and games in Western civilization had traditionally belonged to the elite. Backgammon, for hundreds of years, was one of those games.

After centuries of play within the relatively closed circle of the very leisured class, why now the sudden rush by so many to roll dice and move fifteen stones around a succession of twenty-four points on a board? Frankly, I am surprised it didn't happen before, since backgammon is *the perfect game*, one that rewards skill yet contains an element of luck. The outcome of the game is in doubt until the last roll of the dice.

Most players readily acknowledge that the doubling rule introduced almost half a century ago—probably by a confident player—sparked up backgammon and turned it into the fast-paced highly charged action game that it is. Addition of this gambling device broadened dimensions and assured more interesting games for players and onlooking bettors. The possibility of raised stakes may serve to increase the tension, but it also increases the options.

If one player wishes to double the stakes at any point, and the game is obviously to his advantage, his opponent may end the game and pay whatever the stakes are at that juncture. A new, potentially more viable game can then start. If the advantage in the game keeps shifting, the optional doubling, redoubling, and re-redoubling keep the odds jumping and the stakes spiraling. As the cube multiplies up to sixty-four, one well-bet game can—and often has—accounted for a player's losses or gains for an entire evening. Incredible stories of fortunes won and lost on a single game are a popular part of backgammon banter.

But not everyone wants to gamble fortunes. Backgammon attracts its following on several levels. The game is extremely sociable—if players talk a little, eat a little, drink and gamble a little, that is often all part of the ambience—visually rewarding, and almost always fast. The average contest takes five or six minutes.

Backgammon is now one of the biggest money games in the world. Last year, in the United States alone, over five million dollars' worth of backgammon layouts were sold. These ranged from brass-legged, specially inlaid marble tables priced at several hundred dollars, to standard wooden models costing under ten dollars a set. Checkers, which ordinarily are packaged by the dozen (so more than one set will be needed), and the back side of many dime-store checkerboards can double as inexpensive setups.

The burgeoning popularity of the game is evident in the number of visible tournaments and contests at country clubs, private clubs, resorts, and charity functions, as well as at ski lodges, neighborhood pubs, and in the back rooms of increasing numbers of favorite restaurants and nightclubs.

Trend-watchers claim that backgammon may be one of the greatest two-handed family entertainments yet—whether or not played for real stakes. It offers multiple advantages over the standard alternatives for family enjoyment. Chess calls on pure logic and strategy and can be taxing and time-consuming for both the players and any spectators. And checkers is often too predictable—experts playing one another often can tell from the first moves who will be the victor—or too repetitious. Old family favorites like Scrabble and Monopoly are always lengthy affairs and often reflect age and experience to an unrewarding degree.

But backgammon has the appropriate blend of chance, choice, and speed for the family den. A father and daughter, mother and son, brother and sister—any family permutation—may sit down and play a few games before or after dinner (some family members play almost every night to see who will do the dishes). Backgammon, like ping-pong, is a good round-robin game, with the winner taking on sequential opponents. Since most games take only a few minutes, rarely does one have to go unfinished. And there's usually time for that "just one more."

Backgammon contests have been perennial favorites among families, friends, and strangers, rich and otherwise, in the Middle East and the eastern Mediterranean countries. In Greece and Turkey, backgammon is practically a national pastime. Nearly everyone plays, from shipowners to fishermen, from tour guides to cab-drivers, and the cabbies will often take breaks between fares to toss the dice at *moultezin* and *gioul*, local Turkish variations of the game, or *plakoto* or *eureika*, as the sport is known in Greece.

In Europe, game play attracts international celebrities, their entourages, and others nightly to such places as the Traveler's Club in Paris, the Palace Hotels in St. Moritz and Gstaad, and clubs in other resort cities like Cannes, Monte Carlo, and Lisbon.

For followers of the backgammon circuit, the game offers

glamour, good company, and fulfillment of gambling appetities. Championship stakes at tournaments lure the rich and the talented, some to bet and some to play. In official tournaments, sponsors put up prize money or backers bid for players and split the winnings with them—sometimes both.

Although experts at the game are quick to encourage novices by claiming anyone (with luck as a silent partner) can win, it is imperative for new players to understand that in the long run good dice plus good strategy make for the best bets. Playing well consistently means acquiring subtlety and finesse. These come from playing, particularly with opponents at the same or more proficient level, even if the learner loses in the process at the outset.

To help the novice backgammon player to understand and develop his or her game, *Beginning Backgammon* puts it all together—the basic principles of the game, thorough explanation of the strategies and their possibilities, and lots of sound advice. The next move is yours.

PATTI ROSENFELD

BEGINNING BACKGAMMON

Introduction

LEARNING TO PLAY any game requires effort and concentration —if you want to become more than a mediocre player. Backgammon is no exception.

The learning process can be pleasant or boring, depending on what we make of it. We learn much faster—and better—when learning is fun. I have kept that in mind as I prepared this book.

Let's play backgammon.

And let's have fun!

• • •

The road to *successful* backgammon is, for the most part, traveled more quickly when the beginner starts to play immediately. Let's ignore theories and subtleties until you've learned how to play. These can come later—*after you've learned the game.*

Before we start we'll need:

1

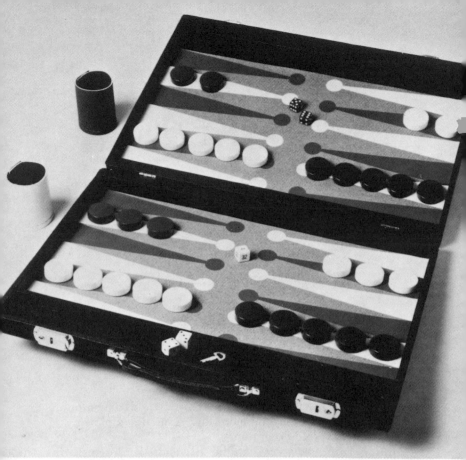

1. *Equipment.*

- A *backgammon board.* (These vary in size and color, as well as cost.)

- *Thirty men* (like checkers)—fifteen of one color and fifteen of another. For the purpose of this book we will use Black and White.

- *Two dice and a dice cup.* (Four dice and two cups are preferable, since it is more enjoyable for each player to have his own.)

- A *doubling block or cube,* which has the numbers 2, 4, 8, 16, 32, and 64 on its sides.

An opponent. Backgammon is played by two people. (A board and men are all you need right now to begin; I will be your opponent.)

2. *An understanding of the set-up of the game.*

The board can be set up in either of the two positions shown in the following diagrams:

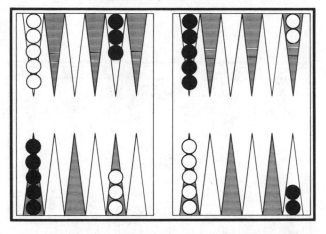

DIAGRAM 1

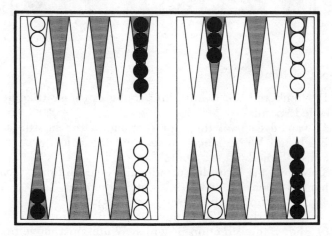

DIAGRAM 2

There are two ways to set up the board. Memorize these diagrams thoroughly, since every game of backgammon that you play will start from one of these two positions. We will use the set-up in Diagram 1 for the remainder of this book, although you should learn to play from the alternative position as well.

The diagram below is the same as Diagram 1,

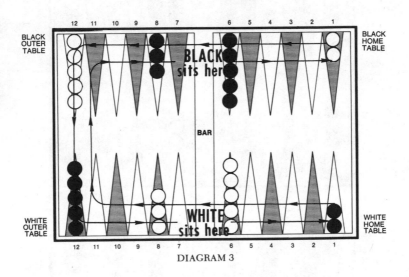

DIAGRAM 3

except that I have:

1) Numbered the twenty-four triangles (these triangles are called "points").
2) Named each of the four sections of the board. (I used Black and White since these were the colors we decided to use throughout the book.)
3) Named the strip that divides the board into its outer and home sections of six triangles each, the "bar."
4) Also named each 7 point, the "bar point."
5) Shown where White must sit and Black must sit.
6) Shown the direction in which White must move his men and the direction in which Black must move his men.

4

3. *The object of the game.*

For White, the object is to move his men around the board in the direction shown in Diagram 3, until all of his men are in White's home board and then bear these men off. Black does the same, only Black moves his men in the opposite direction. The first player to remove all of his men is the winner.

4. *How the game is played.*

The game starts with each player rolling a single die. The player with the higher number showing on his die begins by moving a man or men—his number plus the number rolled by the opponent. In the event both players roll the same number, the players continue to roll a single die until one has a higher number than the other. After the opening roll the players roll alternately with two dice. *(Example)* If White wins the opening roll, on the completion of White's move, it becomes Black's turn to roll. Conversely, if Black rolls the higher number at the start of the game, at the completion of his move it is White's turn to roll.

The men must always be moved *forward* according to the numbers shown on the dice. For example, if your roll is 6 and 1:

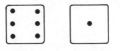

1) You may move one man 6 and then 1 for the full total of 7.
2) One man 1 and then 6, again for the full total of 7.
3) One man 6 and another man 1. The numbers are always taken individually—*never the total.*

(Example) You roll a 5 and a 4.

1) You may move one man 5 and then 4, for a total of 9.
2) You may move one man 4 and then 5, for a total of 9.
3) You may move one man 5 and another man 4.

These rules hold true for every number except doubles. Doubles occur when both dice have the same number showing: two 1's, two 2's, two 3's, etc. In this case the player moves twice the

5

amount shown on the dice. *(Example)* In the case of double 3's, the total shown is 6.

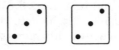

Twice 6 is 12. The 12 may be taken in any of the following ways:

1) One man moves 3, four times.
2) One man moves 3, three times, and a different man 3 once.
3) One man moves 3 two times, and a different man 3 two times.
4) One man moves 3 twice, a different man 3 once, and third man 3 once.
5) Four different men each move 3, once.

It may seem that I've forgotten my promise to get you started playing right away. I haven't. It's just that this is material you must understand and absorb. There is just a bit more before you actually start to move the men.

Stop here for a moment and digest what you have covered so far.

All right, if you're ready, let's go on.

I have explained that the men are moved according to the numbers that show on your dice. However, there is a rule that prohibits a man or men from landing on a point that is occupied by two or more of your opponent's men. (A point is said to be "established" or "made" when a player has two or more men on it.) Other than this, a man or men may land on any other point. If a man or men lands on a point where the opponent has a single man, that single man, or "blot," as we will call him from now on, is taken off the board, and placed on the bar. This is termed a "hit." This blot must start over again by re-entering in his opponent's home board. When a player has one or more men off the board (on the bar), he may make *no* other play until those

6

men are back on the board. He re-enters by throwing, on either of his dice, a number of a point that has not been established by the opponent. There are 6 points on which a player could conceivably re-enter. They are: 1, 2, 3, 4, 5, or 6 point. Since each player starts the game with his 6 point already made, a man who must re-enter early in the game usually must do so on one of the other 5 points.

White may re-enter his man whicn is on the bar by rolling a 1, 2, 3, 4, or 5 on either die—if his roll is 1 & 6 he must enter on Black's one point—if White's roll is 1 & 5 he may choose to enter on either the one or the five point, etc.

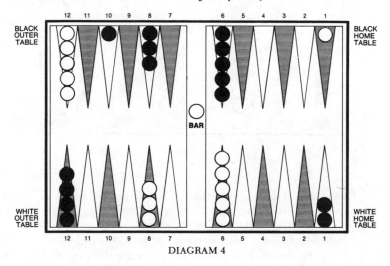

DIAGRAM 4

As the game progresses, your opponent will make more points in his home board, thus making re-entry more difficult.

*Now White may re-enter his man which is on the bar only by roll-
ing a 1, 2, or 4 on either die. If White rolls a 4 he will hit Black's
man and force Black to re-enter White's home board. If White's roll
is 3 & 5, 3 & 6, 5 & 6 or double 3's, 5's or 6's he may not enter.*

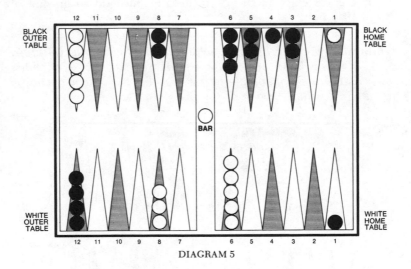

DIAGRAM 5

I've digressed by explaining what happens when a blot is
hit, instead of continuing with the rule that concerns the movement
of men. So let's go back to that for a moment.

I have said that a man or men may be moved to any point
that is not occupied by two or more of your opponent's men.
(In other words—to any point not established or made by your
opponent.)

When you roll a 6 and 5 and move the same man a total
of 11, that man is considered to have moved either a 6 first (landing
momentarily on a space 6 points away from where he started)
and then a 5, or a 5 first (landing momentarily 5 points away
from where he started) and then continuing on for 6 more. In
moving from his original spot to one six away, this man need
not be concerned with any men, his or his opponent's, which
may exist in between. His only concern is the space where he
intends to land.

8

White rolls 6 and 5

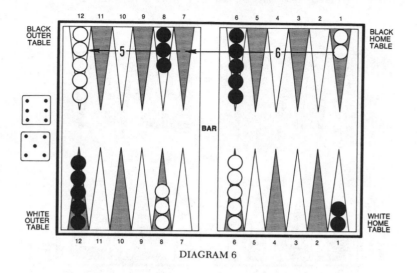

DIAGRAM 6

White's man on Black's 1 point moves 6 to Black's bar point. (He is allowed to land there since Black has not made that point.) This man then moves five more until he reaches Black's 12 point. If you try to move White's man 5 first, and then 6, it won't work, since White would have to land on Black's 6 point—a point that has been made.

Now, let's examine the same roll of 6 and 5, except that the position we will use will be the one shown in Diagram 7.

White rolls 6 and 5.

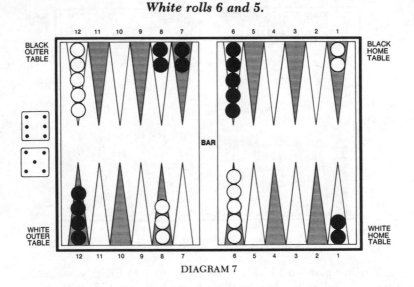

DIAGRAM 7

White cannot move from Black's 1 point, since to do so he would have to start by moving either 6 or 5 and both points where the 6 and 5 would land are occupied by two or more of Black's men. In other words, Black has made both of the points where White must stop in order to make the move.

Perhaps by now you are saying, "Enough of this mumbo-jumbo!"—but don't worry; it will all become clear after you've played a few games.

Here are two more things you should know about how the game works:

When all of your men are in your home board you may start "bearing men off." The rules of "bearing off" seem to be the most difficult for the beginner to absorb. Therefore, I will delay further explanations until they are actually needed.

Finally, you must understand *the winning of the game.*

It is possible to win in three different ways:

1) A simple "win," where you have borne off all of your men and your opponent has borne off at least one man.

10

2) A "gammon," when you have borne off all of your men and your opponent has not borne off any. In this case you will win double the stake you are playing for.

3) A "backgammon," when you have borne off all of your men and your opponent has not borne off any and still has a man or men in your home board or on the bar. In this case you will win triple the stake of the game.

Many things that are confusing to you now will become clear as we go along. Your board should be set up as in Diagram 8.

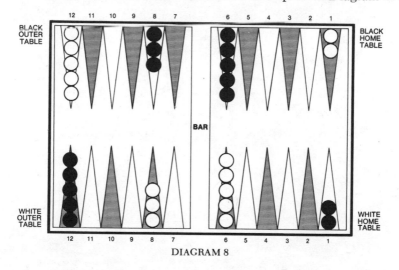

DIAGRAM 8

If you move your men and Black's men as we play each game, you will become familiar with the different moves that are made in the course of the game. You will shorten the time you will be counting the points on the board by touching each one, and you will quickly be able to visualize where a man will land when a given number is rolled.

If you are seated in the right position, let's go!

11

You roll a 6 and Black a 5.

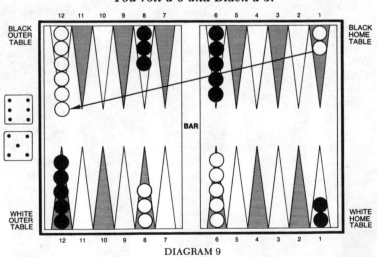

DIAGRAM 9

14

Move one man from Black's 1 point to Black's 12 point. In moving this man the full 11 (the total of the two dice) you actually moved a 6 first and then a 5. When 6 and 5 is the first roll of the game it is always moved in this fashion. Since your objective is to move your men around the board and finally into your home board, the two men that start on your opponent's 1 point are the men that have to travel the farthest; thus you have moved one of the two most difficult men to move, to an established point of your own. From there it is only a short distance to get into your home board. It is now Black's turn, and he rolls 6 and 1.

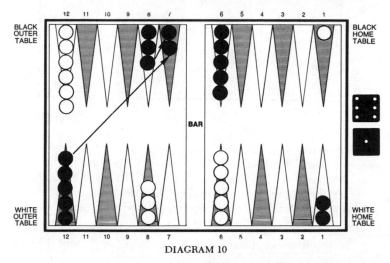

DIAGRAM 10

Moves one man 6 points from your 12 point to Black's bar point and one man 1 point from Black's 8 point to his bar point. Black has now made his bar point. This move serves two purposes. It blocks your man on his 1 point from moving 6 (according to the rule whereby a man or men may not land on a point that is occupied by two or more men of your opponent's). It also creates a landing spot for Black's men to move to without the possibility of being hit by the remaining man you have on this 1 point.

15

White rolls 3 and 1.

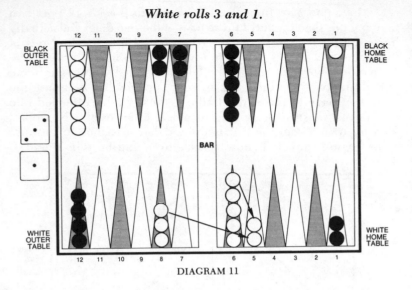

DIAGRAM 11

Move one man 3 points from your 8 point to your 5 point and one man 1 from your 6 point to your 5 point.

You have now made your 5 point. This is a favorable roll early in the game, since it makes the most important point in your home board. This point serves several purposes:

1) It blocks your opponent's men from landing on that point;
2) It will make it more difficult for your opponent if he must re-enter your board; and
3) It serves as a landing spot for any additional men you may wish to move to that point.

Black now rolls 5 and 4.

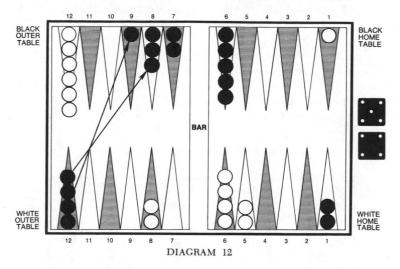

DIAGRAM 12

Move one man 5 from your 12 point to Black's 8 point and one man 4 from your 12 point to Black's 9 point. As you can see, Black has left a blot (a single man which is vulnerable to being hit). Black perhaps would have preferred to use the 4 by moving a man from your 1 point to your 5 point rather than from your 12 point to his 9 point. But this was impossible due to your established 5 point. You can see the value of establishing points in your home board. This will also apply to other points around the board.

Black might have made an alternative use of the 4 by moving a man from his 6 point to his 2 point. However, this would have exposed a blot which would have been vulnerable to being hit if White rolled a 1 on White's next roll, or until Black joins another man with that blot.

Your question now should be: Why is the blot on the 9 point preferable to a blot on the 2 point? To answer this question it will be necessary for you to understand odds and the laws of probability. You are not ready for this yet, so I will simply answer that it is more difficult to hit a blot that is more than 6 points away from the man with which you hope to hit than it is to hit a blot 6 or less away. One more reason for the move to the 9

17

point rather than to the 2 point is that, if the man on the 9 point is hit and sent back to re-enter your home board, Black will have lost 16 points—the amount he will have to roll to get that man back to where he was when he was hit. This amount is arrived at by counting the number of points, starting at White's 1 point to Black's 9 point. If the blot on the Black's 2 point were hit, by using the above system you can see that he would have lost 23 points. The difference is 7 points. Since the average roll of the dice is 8 and a fraction, there is practically a full roll difference in the loss.

White rolls double 5's.

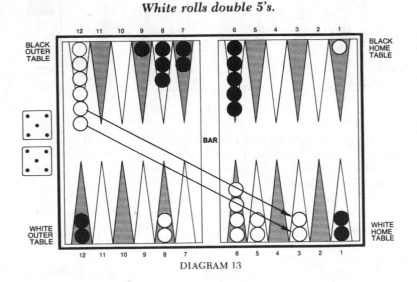

DIAGRAM 13

Move two men from White's 8 point to White's 3 point and two men from Black's 12 point to White's 8 point. (Moving two men from Black's 12 point to White's 3 point is exactly the same.)

Actually, the only other choice of moves for White would have been to move four men from Black's 12 point to White's 8 point. This play is inferior to the one you made because it would fail to make the 3 point in White's home board—which, as you learned when you made your 5 point, is very valuable. It would also put six men on your 8 point. It is now time to tell you that, if possible, you should avoid putting too many men on the same point.

18

The reason for the limited choice was that none of White's other men could be moved. White's blot on Black's 1 point could not move 5 since Black has made his 6 point. The four men on White's 6 point cannot move 5, because Black started with, and still has, White's 1 point made. The two men on White's 5 point cannot move 5, since there isn't room to do so. (The only way to move them 5 would be to take them off the board, and that is not permissible until *all* of White's men are in White's home board.)

Black rolls 5 and 2.

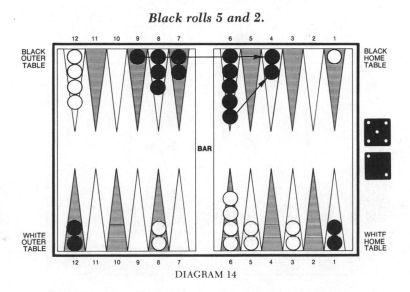

DIAGRAM 14

Make Black's 4 point by moving the blot on Black's 9 point to Black's 4 point and one man from Black's 6 point to Black's 4 point. You should be able to list some of the reasons why this is a good play.

If you said it is good because it established a point which is important because—

1) It blocks White's man on Black's 1 point from moving forward 3 points;
2) It makes it more difficult for White to re-enter Black's board if Black were to hit a blot of White's;

19

3) It established a safe landing spot for other Black men;
4) And because it eliminates the blot on the 9 point, which was vulnerable to being hit

—*you have answered correctly.* If you didn't get all of the first three reasons, go back and start the game again, and *re-read my explanations for each move.* Don't worry—we'll wait here for you. We all could use a breather at this point.

I forgot to mention earlier that the 4 point early in the game is the *second* most valuable point in your home board. (You remember that the 5 point was the *first* most important point.)

If everyone is ready, back to the game.

White rolls 6 and 2.

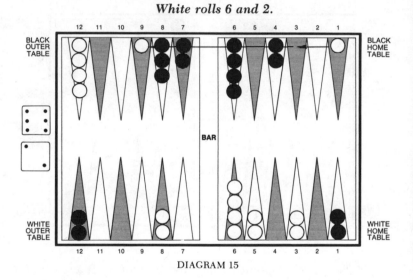

DIAGRAM 15

Move one man 2 and then 6 from Black's 1 point to Black's 9 point. If White's blot is not hit by Black (as you can see, Black needs a 4 to hit), White is then in a position to move that blot to safety on White's next roll. The chances are less than even that Black will hit White. (More about odds and chances later.) It was becoming imperative that White attempt to move this man out of Black's board because Black was beginning to block all of the escape exits. White was able to move only 1's, 2's, and 4's, since Black has blocked 3's, 5's, and 6's. If White had not moved this man and Black's next roll were 3 and 1, which would make his 5 point, White would then have been able to move this man past Black's block only if White rolled a 2 and a 6. The odds against a 2 and 6 are 17 to 1. (I'll show you how to calculate odds after this game has been completed.) An alternative play might have been to move one man from Black's 12 point to White's 5 point. Although this play is safer (it does not expose a blot), the attempted escape of the blot on Black's 1 point takes priority.

Black rolls double 6's.

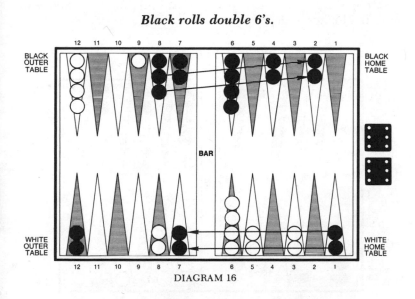

DIAGRAM 16

Move two men from White's 1 point to White's bar point, and two men from Black's 8 point to Black's 2 point.

This is an excellent roll for Black. It enables Black to move his two men out of White's board to a position where greater freedom of movement will be possible on future rolls. As was the case of White's blot on Black's 1 point a moment ago, Black's two men on White's 1 point were in danger of being completely blocked from movement out of White's board. Black, by establishing White's bar, has also created a block which White will have difficulty in circumventing. It would have been wrong for Black to use the other two 6's by moving his men from White's 12 point

21

to Black's bar point, because the two men remaining on White's 12 point serve a dual purpose. They constitute a landing spot for the two men now on White's bar and they are also a block to White's men which have not moved past this point.

With his last two 6's, Black had the choice of either moving the men he actually moved or moving two men from his bar point to his 1 point. Both moves establish a point. However, when you have a choice as to which point to make and do not have to worry about leaving blots as a result of your move (when there no longer is an opponent's man or men which can hit you), it is better to make the higher of the two points.

White rolls 6 and 2.

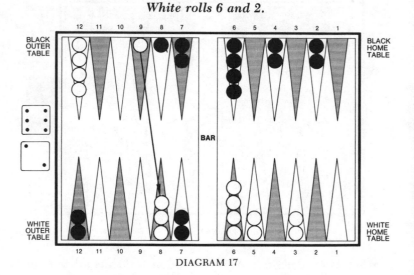

DIAGRAM 17

Move White's blot from Black's 9 point to White's 8 point. If you would have made this move, very good—you are getting the idea quickly. This roll enabled White to bring his blot to the safety of an established point. White now only has to bring his seven remaining men (four on Black's 12 point and three on White's 8 point) into White's home board before he is able to start the bearing off process. Of White's seven remaining men, the four on Black's 12 point have to move past two of Black's blocks, the block on White's 12 point and the block on White's

22

bar point. The other three men (those on White's bar point) have to get past only one block, Black's men on White's bar point. These three men will be much easier to move to safety into White's home board than the first four, since any die rolled by White which is 2 or higher will enable White to move into his home board. Looking forward and trying to anticipate what problems you, as White, may have in your attempt to be victorious, you can see that the movement of these four men on Black's 12 point is your biggest concern.

By the way, file the term, "anticipating future moves" away in your mind—it is the cornerstone of good backgammon. In very little time, and all by yourself, you will be "anticipating future moves."

Black rolls 3 and 2.

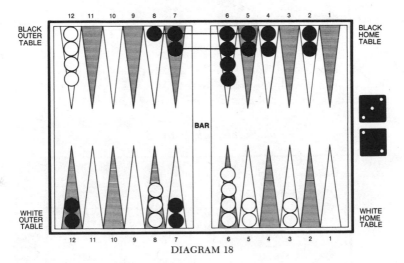

DIAGRAM 18

Make Black's 5 point by moving one man from Black's bar to Black's 5 point. This point has lost much of its importance to Black, since it is like locking the barn door after the horse is gone. However, in the event that White in his attempt to get his men into his home board leaves a blot that Black is fortunate enough to hit, then, as we discussed before, the 5 point will reassume its importance, since it will prevent White from re-entering Black's home board on the 5 point.

White rolls 5 and 3.

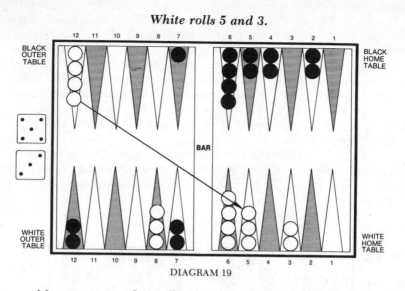

DIAGRAM 19

Move one man from Black's 12 point to White's 8 point and then continue with the same man to White's 5 point. That's one less man to worry about since he is now safe in White's home board.

Black rolls 2 and 1.

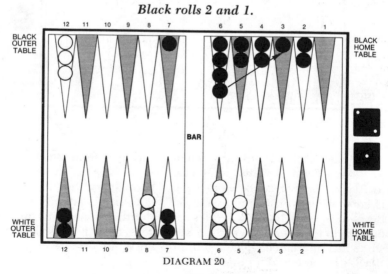

DIAGRAM 20

24

Move one man two from Black's 6 point to Black's 4 point and then one to Black's 3 point. Black is starting to make his 3 point and he is also putting a man on a blank space so that, when the time comes to bear off, his men will be more evenly distributed.

White rolls double 4's.

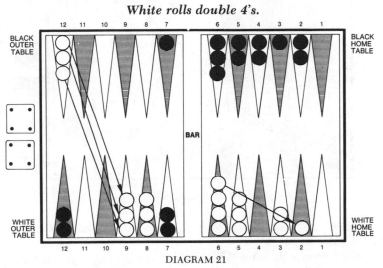

DIAGRAM 21

(What a delightful roll!)

Move three men (the men we decided were our biggest problem) from Black's 12 point to White's 9 point and one man from White's 6 point to White's 2 point. This last move, from the 6 point to the 2 point, was made in preference to bringing one man from the outer board to the home board. The reason may be a little advanced for you at this moment, but, since you will eventually have to learn it, it may as well be now. If you had brought one man from the outer board to the home board, a total of five men would remain in your outer board. If on your next turn you rolled double 6's, you would be forced to move four of these men into your home board. This would leave a blot that Black's men on your bar would be able to hit. If this blot were hit, it would have to re-enter Black's home board and then move all the way around the board once again. This would be an unnecessary risk, and all possible precautions should be taken to avoid it.

25

Black rolls 6 and 4.

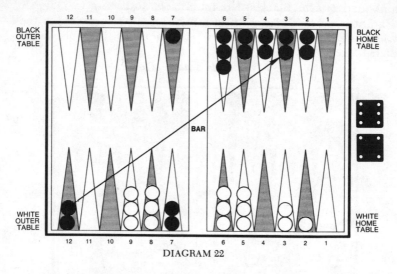

DIAGRAM 22

Move one man 6 from White's 12 point to Black's bar, and then 4 more to Black's 3 point.

Black is now behind White in the race to get their men into their home board. If the rolls were equal from here to the end of the game White would win. Black must hope to get a chance to hit one of White's men. This hope is rather slim, since White's movement into his home board is restricted only by Black's block on White's bar point. Nevertheless, if White does leave a blot and Black does hit, Black's home board is now impregnable except for the 1 point.

White rolls double 6's.

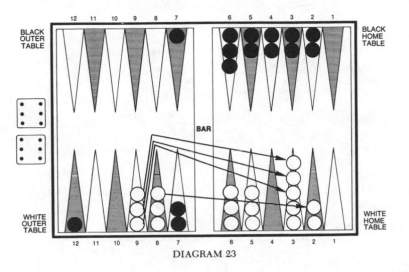

DIAGRAM 23

(Ah-ha—I'm glad we took those precautions on the last roll!)

Move three men from White's 9 point to White's 3 point, and one man from White's 8 point to White's 2 point.

Three men from White's 9 point were moved in preference to three men from White's 8 point, because the two remaining men on White's 8 point will be easier to move into White's home board than the two men on White's 9 point. All numbers rolled except 1's move in safely from the 8 point, whereas all numbers except 1's and 2's move in from the 9 point.

Black rolls 6 and 5.

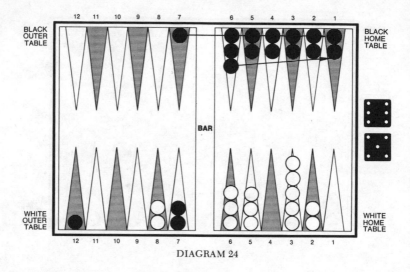

DIAGRAM 24

Move one man from Black's bar point to Black's 1 point and one man from Black's 6 point to Black's 1 point. This makes Black's 1 point, and, in backgammon terminology, it gives Black a "closed board"—all the points have been made. This means that if a blot or blots of White's were hit it would be impossible for White to re-enter Black's board, since a blot when hit must re-enter the opponent's home board on any of the points from 1 to 6 that is not occupied by two or more of the opponent's men.

28

White rolls 6 and 4.

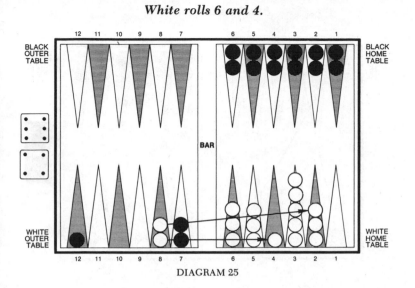

DIAGRAM 25

Move one man from White's 8 point to White's 4 point and one man from White's 8 point to White's 2 point. You now have all of your men in your home board and are ready to start the bearing off process on your next roll.

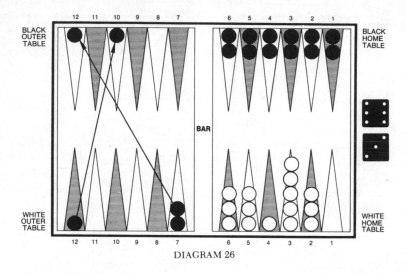

DIAGRAM 26

Move one man from White's bar to Black's 12 point and one man from White's 12 point to Black's 10 point. Black's objective now is to move his men as quickly as possible into his home board so that he also can start bearing off.

Time out for a bit of information concerning movement when all of your men have passed all of your opponent's men—that is, when no further "contact" is possible.

A player should try to move his men from board to board —Black's outer to your outer, your outer to your home, etc.—with the least amount of wasted numbers. The man Black moved from White's bar to Black's 12 point moved from White's outer board to Black's outer board without wasting a single number. (Any number less than a 6 would not have crossed from one board to the other.) The man that moved 3 points from White's 12 point to Black's 10 point also crossed from one board to another, but a 1 would have accomplished the same thing. Therefore, the extra 2 points were basically unnecessary. Some of the time it will be difficult to find a man that will go from one board to another without wasting some points. The objective is to move with the least waste. Had Black moved the man on White's 12 point six to Black's bar point, the waste would have been 5 points, because

30

a 1 would have been sufficient to cross from White's outer board to Black's outer board. In case this is confusing, consider the two examples below.

There will be more for you to learn about this part of the game, but for our purposes now this much will be adequate.

Black rolls 6 and 1.

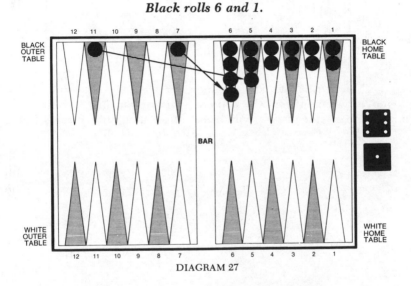

DIAGRAM 27

Move the man on Black's 11 point 6 to Black's 5 point and the man on Black's bar to Black's 6. If you moved the man on Black's 11 point 1 and the man on Black's bar 6, you would be wasting 5 points, since the man on Black's bar needed only a 1 to cross from board to board. In addition, only one man will have moved from board to board instead of two.

31

Black rolls double 6's.

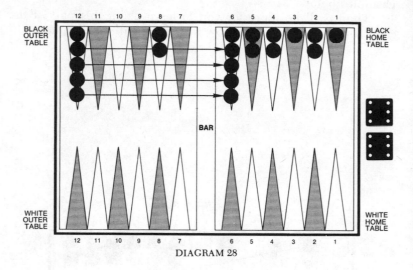

DIAGRAM 28

You must move all four men from Black's 12 point. If you move two men from the 8 point you are wasting 4 points with each man since two's will bring these men into Black's home board.

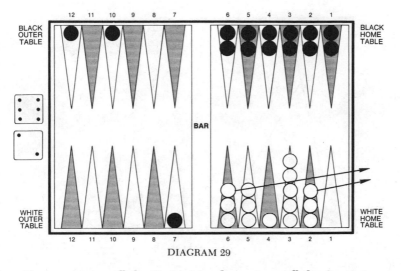

DIAGRAM 29

Bear one man off the 6 point, and one man off the 2 point.

Sorry, but before we move on you will have to understand the rules concerning bearing off—the rules we postponed earlier.

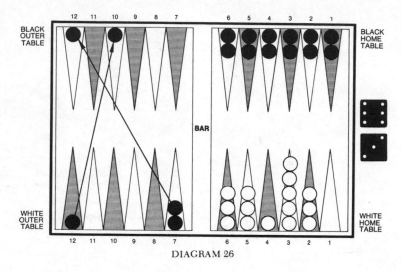

DIAGRAM 26

The points in your home board are numbered from 1 to 6. As you see in Diagram 26, your fifteen men are in your home board and are ready to be borne off. These men are taken off according to the numbers you roll.

1) If your roll is 6 and a 2, you may bear a man off from the 6 point and one man from the 2 point. If your roll is 4 and 2, you may take one man off your 4 point, and one man off your 2 point. If your roll is 4 and 3, you may take one man off your 4 point and one man off your 3 point, and so on.

2) If your roll is a double, you may take twice the amount shown on the dice. For example if your roll is double 3's, you may take four men off the 3 point.

You roll 6 and 2.

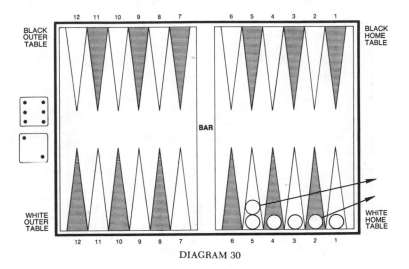

DIAGRAM 30

You roll double 6's.

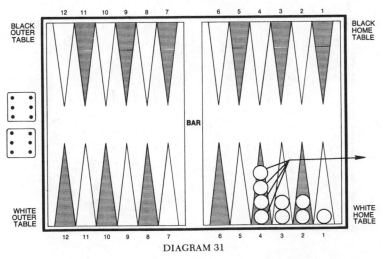

DIAGRAM 31

35

You roll double 5's.

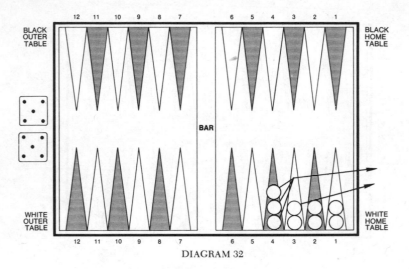

DIAGRAM 32

You roll double 6's.

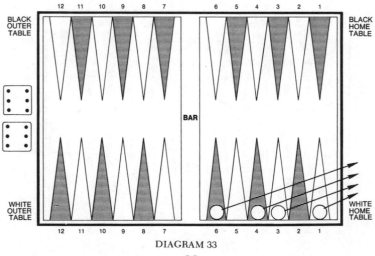

DIAGRAM 33

36

3) If your roll is 6 and 2, and you have no men on your 6 point, you may take a man off the next highest point your men are on and a man from your 2 point.

In general, if you roll a number that is higher than any point upon which you have a man, you merely consider that number as the number of the next highest point upon which you do have a man or men. This also applies with doubles. For example, if your board looks like this and your roll is double 6's, you may bear four men off your 4 point. In other words, the 6's are considered as double 4's. In another example, when your roll is double 5's, you take three men off the 4 point and one man from the 3 point. One more example: You have but four men left on the board and you roll double 6's. Take all four men off. The use of the first of your four 6's leaves the man on the 4 point the highest occupied point, so you consider the second 6 a 4. After the man on the four is removed, the man on the 3 point is the next highest occupied point and you use your third 6 as if it were a 3. Finally, you do the same with the man on the 1 point.

4) It is not necessary to bear men off if you can. You may, if you desire to, move forward in your board, using one number to bear a man off and the other to move forward, or using both numbers to move forward.

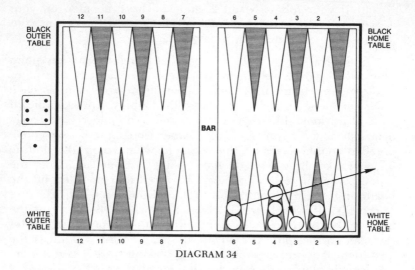

DIAGRAM 34

If you roll a 6 and 1, you may bear off the man from the 6 point and then move one man forward from the 4 point to the 3 point, rather than taking a man off the 1 point.

You may use both numbers to move forward in the inner board. This becomes important when your opponent has a man or men in your board and you do not wish to leave a blot. More about this later, but remember that the men do not necessarily have to be borne off—they can be moved forward.

5) When you roll a number where you do not have a man. In this case you are forced to move forward.

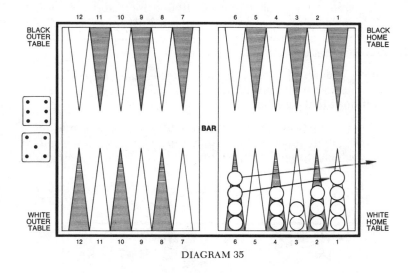

DIAGRAM 35

(Example 1) You roll 6 and 5. You take one man off the 6 point and move one man 5 from the 6 point to the 1 point.

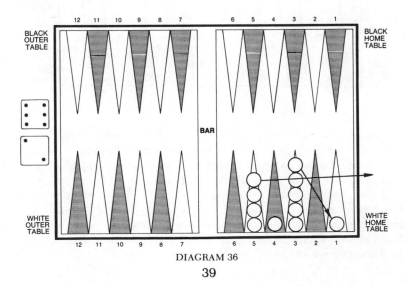

DIAGRAM 36

39

(Example 2) You have borne off five men and now roll 6 and 2. You have no men on the 6 point. Take one man off the next occupied point, the 5 point, and move one man from the 3 point 2 points down to the 1 point.

6) If you are hit while bearing off, the man or men hit must re-enter your opponent's home board. You then may not bear off until that man has returned to your home board.

Don't be too concerned if Egyptian hieroglyphics would seem simple in comparison to the paragraphs you have just read. It will become decipherable in no time at all. Now, back to our game!

Black rolls 6 and 4.

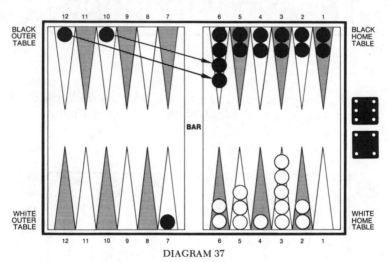

DIAGRAM 37

Move one man from Black's 12 point to Black's 6 point and one man from Black's 10 point to Black's 6 point, both men moving from Black's outer to home board without a wasted number. Had you moved the man from Black's 12 point four to Black's 8 point and the man on Black's 10 point six to Black's 4 point, this 6-point movement would have wasted two numbers: a 4 would have crossed from Black's outer to home board, and only one man would have moved from one board to another, rather than two men as in the move we chose to make.

40

White rolls 5 and 3.

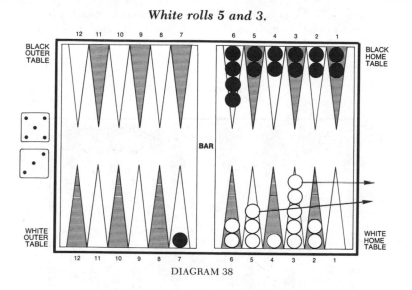

DIAGRAM 38

Bear one man off White's 5 point and one man from White's 2 point. (Again, this is simple.)

Black rolls 5 and 4.

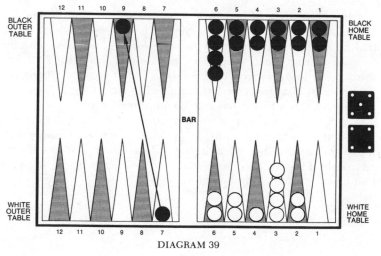

DIAGRAM 39

41

Move Black's man from White's bar point to Black's 9 point. We must have this man in Black's home board before Black can start bearing off.

White rolls 5 and 1.

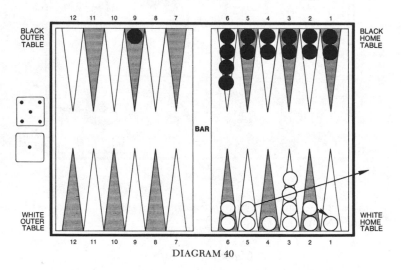

DIAGRAM 40

Bear one man off White's 5 point and move one man from White's 2 point to White's 1 point. (The five was easy.) As you had no man on the 1 point, you were forced to move some man forward in the board. You therefore moved from the 2 point to the 1 point in order to put a man on a blank space. This insured the removal of at least two men on White's next roll, since every space in White's board has one or more men on it.

Assuming your opponent has no men in your home board with which to hit you—and, in general, when you are forced to move forward, rather than being able to bear a man off—it is advisable if possible to move to a space which is blank or a space that has the fewest number of men.

Black rolls 4 and 2.

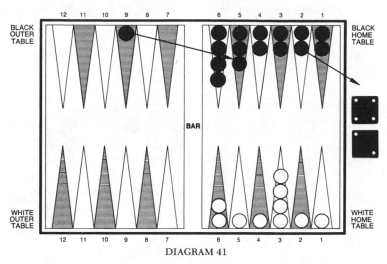

DIAGRAM 41

Move the man from Black's 9 point to Black's 5 point and bear off one man from Black's 2 point.

White rolls double 6's.

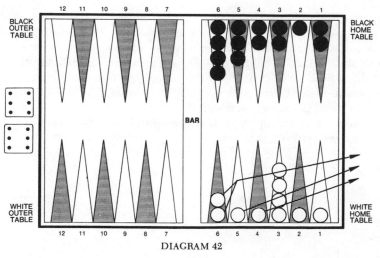

DIAGRAM 42

43

Bear off two men from White's 6 point, one man from White's 5 point, and one man from White's 4 point. There were only two actual 6's; therefore we considered the third 6 a 5, and then the fourth 6 as a 4. (Fret not—you'll get used to it!)

Black rolls double 3's.

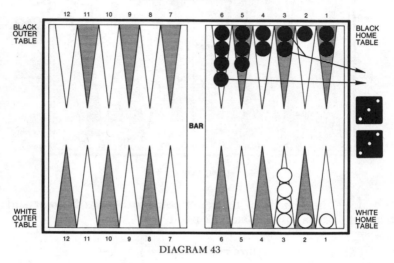

DIAGRAM 43

Bear two men off Black's 3 point and one man from Black's 6 point. After using two of your four 3's to bear the men off your 3 point, you still had two left to play, so the man which you bore off Black's 6 point actually moved forward 3 points and then off the 3 point, which used up the remaining two 3's. NOTE: For the remainder of this book we will substitute the word "pips" for the word points when discussing the amount of spaces a man is moved. For example, instead of "moving a man forward 3 points," we will now say "moving a man forward 3 pips."

44

White rolls 6 and 4.

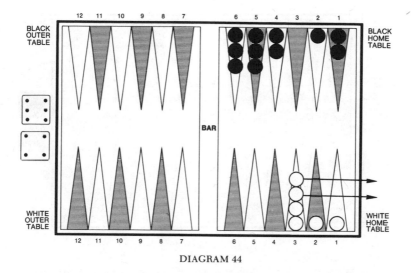

DIAGRAM 44

Since we have no men on either the 6, 5, or 4 point, we must consider the 6 as a three and the 4 as a three. (This is not considered a double, of course, as a double occurs only when the dice actually show the same numbers.) Therefore, bear two men off the 3 point.

Black rolls 4 and 1.

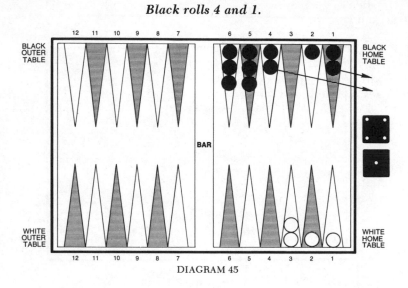

DIAGRAM 45

Bear one man off Black's 4 point and one man off Black's 1 point. (It's getting easier—yes?)

White rolls 6 and 1.

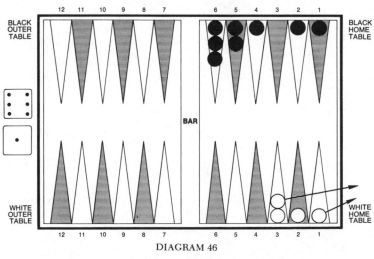

DIAGRAM 46

Bear one man off the 3 point and one man off the 1 point. (The 6 is considered as a 3.)

It should be obvious that White will be the victor in this particular game. As a matter of fact, White *was* the winner prior to this last roll. It is not necessary that you recognize this now; it will be explained later. Once you understand and this situation arises, you will end the game without further ado.

Let's finish, nevertheless, since it will help by giving you a little more experience in bearing off.

Black rolls double 5's.

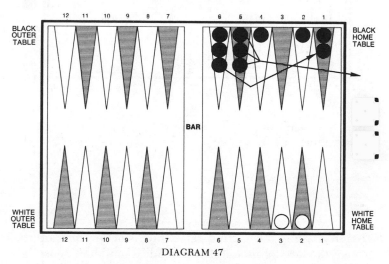

DIAGRAM 47

Bear three men off Black's 5 point and move one man forward from Black's 6 point to Black's 1 point.

Since we did not have a fourth five, we were forced to move the man forward from the 6 point.

47

White rolls 4 and 2.

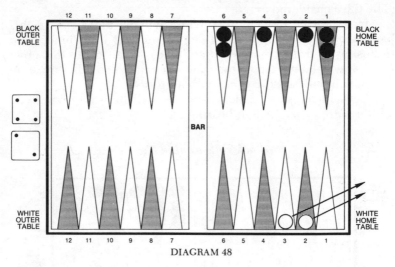

DIAGRAM 48

Bear one man from the 3 point and one man from the 2 point.
Congratulations! You have played—*and won*—your first game of backgammon.

Before starting our second game, this is an appropriate time to explain the laws of probability and odds—and how those laws apply to backgammon. Once you have a working knowledge of the general concept of backgammon, many of the moves that you will make in future games, moves that can be played in one of several ways, will be influenced by your understanding of odds and probabilities. For those of you who understand the information I am about to give, take this time to go back and play the previous game from its start to its conclusion.

For the others, put on your thinking caps!

There are 36 possible combinations of rolls on the dice in backgammon. This figure is arrived at by multiplying the 6 numbers on one die by the 6 numbers on the second die. The following chart lists these possible combinations.

48

36 Combinations of the Dice

Double 1	1
Double 2	1
Double 3	1
Double 4	1
Double 5	1
Double 6	1
1 and 2, or 2 and 1	2
1 and 3, or 3 and 1	2
1 and 4, or 4 and 1	2
1 and 5, or 5 and 1	2
1 and 6, or 6 and 1	2
2 and 3, or 3 and 2	2
2 and 4, or 4 and 2	2
2 and 5, or 5 and 2	2
2 and 6, or 6 and 2	2
3 and 4, or 4 and 3	2
3 and 5, or 5 and 3	2
3 and 6, or 6 and 3	2
4 and 5, or 5 and 4	2
4 and 6, or 6 and 4	2
5 and 6, or 6 and 5	2

TOTAL   36

If you examine this chart you will see that fifteen combinations occur twice. For example, let's assume that one die is red and the second die is green. The combination 1 and 6 occurs when the green die has a 1 and the red die shows 6, and also when the red die shows a 1 and green die shows a 6. The same is true of all other combinations. The fifteen combinations that occur twice account for 30 of the 36 possible combinations—the remaining 6 are doubles, which occur only once each. Therefore, a specific combination such as 6 and 1 should occur, on the average, twice in every 36 rolls. This will hold true for any other specific combination, with the exception of doubles. A specific double has a probability of occurring only one time out of 36.

If I now asked you what are the chances of rolling a 6 and 1, you should answer two times in 36. Or, expressed another way, there are 34 chances *against* rolling 6 and 1 versus two chances to roll a 6 and 1. We might further simplify this

49

by saying that the odds are 17 to 1 against it occurring. We arrived at 17 to 1 by dividing the number of chances against (34) by the number of chances for (2), and reducing this by the lowest common denominator: $\frac{34}{2}$ or $\frac{17}{1}$.

We now know that the odds of rolling *any specific combination* (6 and 1, 6 and 2, 5 and 3, 4 and 2, etc.) is 17 to 1 against it happening.

Since any specific double (two 1's, two 2's, etc.) occurs but one time in 36 rolls, this means that 35 times it will not. Or simplified, the odds are 35 to 1 against a specific double occurring.

Let me now explain how this information might apply to backgammon.

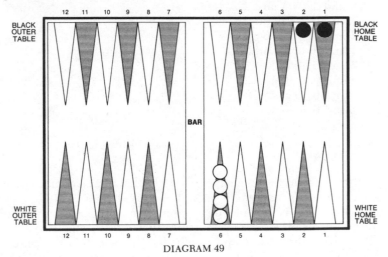

DIAGRAM 49

Look at Diagram 49, both Black and White are bearing off. It is your roll (remember, throughout this book you are White), and you want to know what are your chances of winning this game. All right, let's answer that.

Since Black, on his next turn to roll, will automatically bear off both of his remaining men, he will win unless White bears off all four of the men on White's 6 point before Black can roll. To do this White must roll double 6's; and, since we know that a specific double occurs only once in 36 times, we can say that White's chances of winning this game are 35 to 1 against.

50

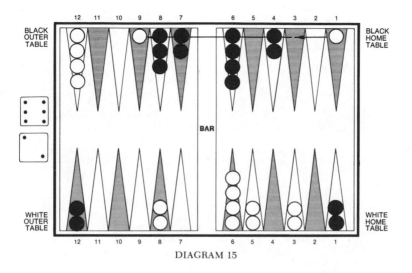

DIAGRAM 15

Back in Diagram 15 in our first game, after White moved his 6 and 2 and Black needed a 4 to hit White's blot, I said that Black's chances of hitting this blot were "less than even." Now, using your new table, I will show you how I arrived at that conclusion.

You can see that a 4 occurs 11 different times in the table (1 and 4, 4 and 1, 2 and 4, 4 and 2, 3 and 4, 4 and 3, 4 and 4, 5 and 4, 4 and 5, 6 and 4, and 4 and 6). To this we must add 3 and 1, 1 and 3, and double 2's, since these are alternative ways of rolling a four. Double 1's also would be a four, but, since it cannot be moved due to Black's 12 point, it is a combination that cannot be added in your calculations. So you are left with eleven combinations of fours plus two of 3 and 1 and one of double 2's, giving a total of 14 possible combinations out of 36 with which Black can hit your blot. Since 18 out of 36 would be an *even* chance, 14 out of 36 makes it *better than even* that your blot will not be hit.

There are more facts about odds and probabilities that you will have to learn, but we'll hold those till later. Right now, let's start Game Two.

GAME TWO

Black rolls 3 and White rolls 1.

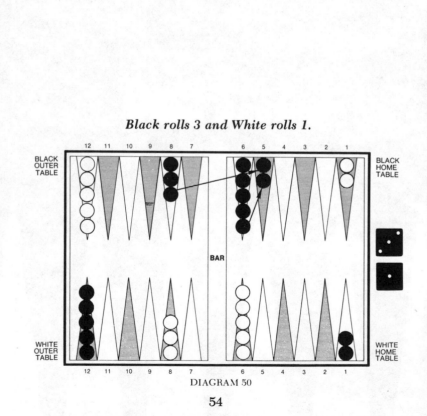

DIAGRAM 50

Move one man from Black's 8 point to Black's 5 point and one man from Black's 6 point to Black's 5 point. From now on, with this roll, I'll merely say "Make Black's 5 point"—and you *should* know which men to move.

You learned in Game One that the 5 point is the most valuable in your home board. At all times you will make the 5 point with an opening roll of 3 and 1.

Let's digress for a moment here.

There are fifteen possible opening rolls. This is information you learned from the table that showed the thirty-six possible combinations that could be rolled. Since it is not possible to start a game with doubles, that leaves thirty combinations, and you discovered that the remaining thirty are fifteen numbers, which are repeated twice. So there are fifteen possible opening rolls.

I have told you that 6 and 5, and 3 and 1, are played in the same way every time. To these, I'm going to add 4 and 2, and 6 and 1.

Examine the following diagrams—*commit them to memory.*

First, 6 and 5:

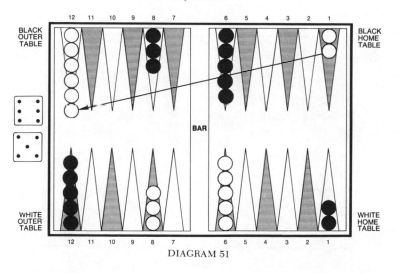

DIAGRAM 51

The roll 6 and 5 is a good one. (Check back with my explanation for Game One.)

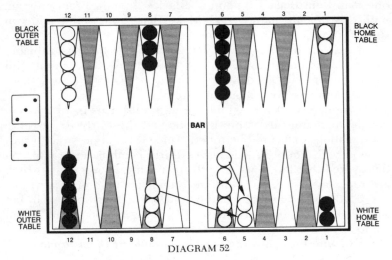

DIAGRAM 52

Third, 4 and 2:

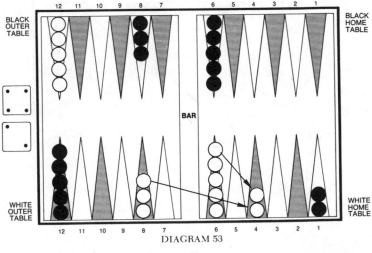

DIAGRAM 53

And fourth, 6 and 1:

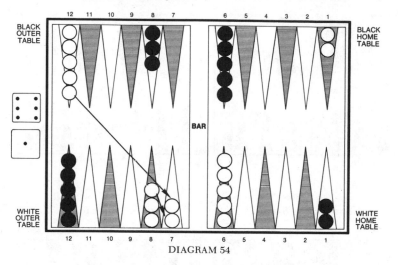

DIAGRAM 54

A short explanation is necessary here for 3 and 1, since you should remember the more lengthy analysis in Game One of White's early (admittedly, not *opening*) 3 and 1 roll. This is a good roll because it creates a block against the opponent, it creates a safe landing spot, and it will make it more difficult for your opponent to re-enter in the event one of his blots is hit.

As for 4 and 2, it's good for the same reasons as 3 and 1.

And 6 and 1—same as 3 and 1, 4 and 2, with the exception of having an effect on your opponent's re-entry.

These four opening rolls are the only rolls that are always played in the same fashion. They also happen to be the most advantageous.

Each of the remaining eleven rolls may be played in one or more ways that I find perfectly acceptable. The difference is simply that of a conservative versus an aggressive approach. With the aggressive moves, the possible gains are greater than those with the conservative approach. The risks involved, however, are commensurate. Before deciding which style you are going to adopt, play for a while—trying both approaches—and then decide. You may discover that you have an instinctive preference for one or the other, or you may choose a mixed style. Remember, whichever you choose, they are all *correct*. I, myself, vary according to my opposition and my mood at the time.

Aggressive 6 and 2.

Aggressive 6 and 3.

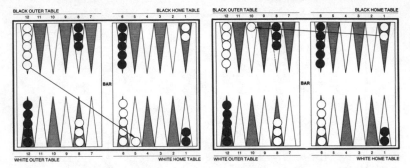

Conservative 6 and 2.

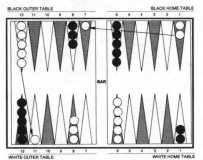

Conservative 6 and 3.

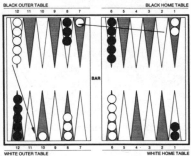

Alternate 6 and 2.

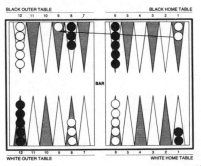

No Alternate

Aggressive 6 and 4.

Aggressive 5 and 1.

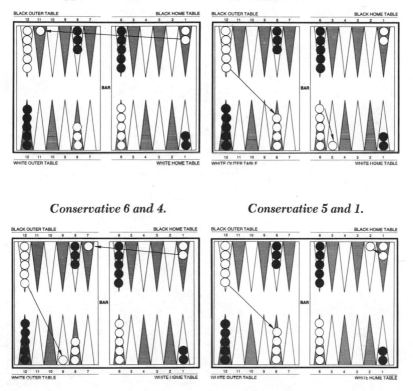

Conservative 6 and 4.

Conservative 5 and 1.

Alternate 6 and 4.

Alternate 5 and 1.

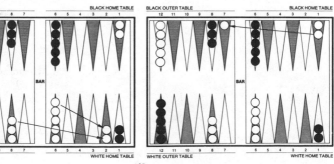

Only Correct Move 5 and 2.

Aggressive 5 and 3.

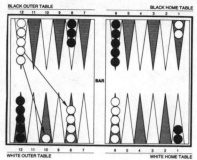

Conservative 5 and 3.

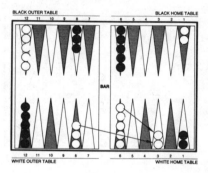

No Alternate

Aggressive 5 and 4.

Aggressive 4 and 1.

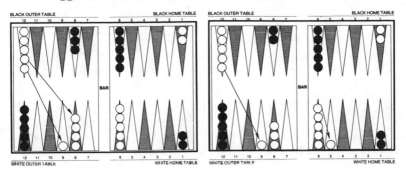

Conservative 5 and 4.

Conservative 4 and 1.

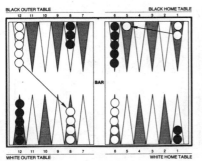
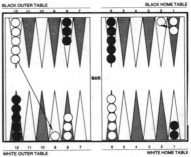

Alternate 5 and 4.

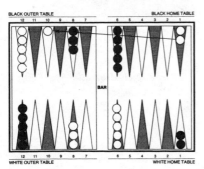

No Alternate

61

Aggressive 4 and 3.

Aggressive 3 and 2.

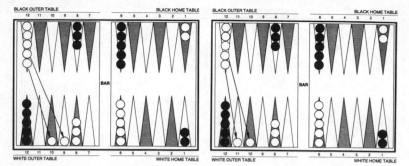

Conservative 4 and 3.

Conservative 3 and 2.

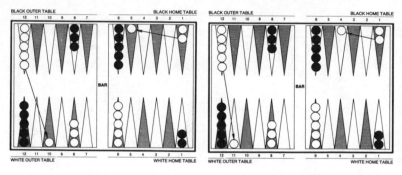

Alternate 4 and 3.

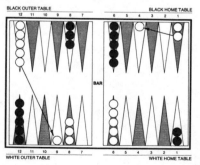

No Alternate

Aggressive 2 and 1.

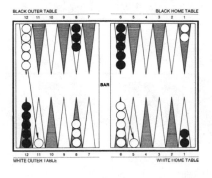

Conservative 2 and 1.

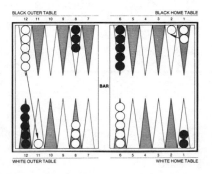

No Alternate

63

A short time ago we started Game Two, with Black having an opening roll of 3 and 1 to make his 5 point. Let us proceed.

White rolls 5 and 3.

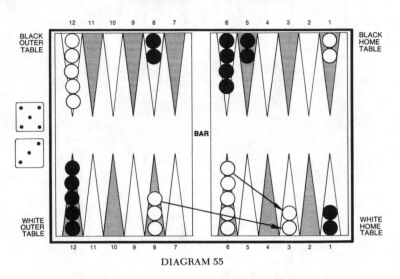

DIAGRAM 55

Make White's 3 point. I choose to make the 3 point rather than moving two men from Black's 12 point—one to White's 10 point and one to White's 8 point—because Black has made a second point in his board. Therefore I feel that White should also make a second point rather than risk having a blot being hit.

Black rolls 4 and 2.

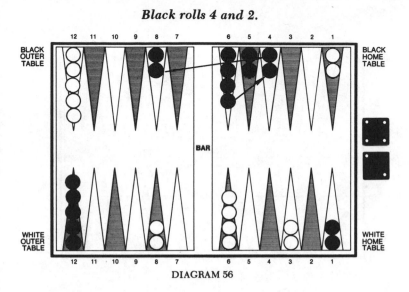

DIAGRAM 56

Make Black's 4 point. There are no correct alternative moves, although Black has exposed a blot which could be hit by White's rolling a 1 and 6 or a 2 and 5. The odds are 8 to 1 against this happening (1 and 6 occurs twice, and 2 and 5 occurs twice—a total of four chances out of 36, or *eight to one against*). Try to become accustomed to figuring the odds yourselves.

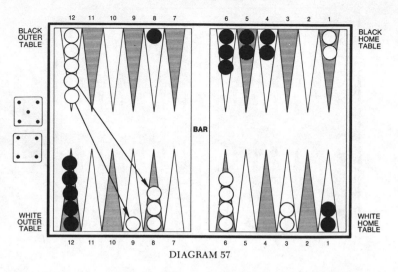

DIAGRAM 57

Move one man from Black's 12 point to White's 8 point and one man from Black's 12 point to White's 9 point.

White is hoping to make either his bar, 5, or 4 point on his next roll. The extra man on White's 8 point (you need only two men to make a point) is termed a "builder."

66

Black rolls 6 and 2.

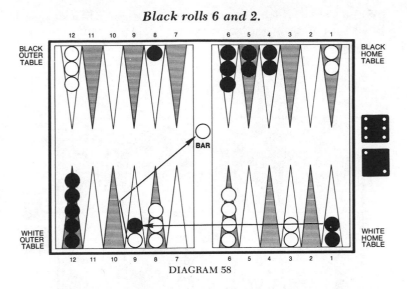

DIAGRAM 58

Move one man 6 and 2 from White's 1 point and hit White's blot on White's 9 point. Take White's man off the table, putting him "on the bar."

White rolls 1 and 4.

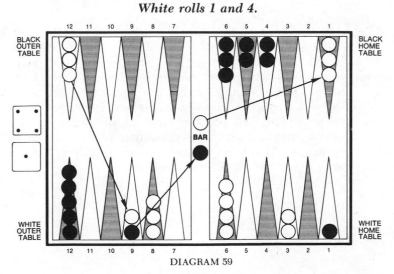

DIAGRAM 59

67

White's man, which was on the Bar, must enter Black's board on Black's 1 point, since Black's 4 point is closed. Move one man from Black's 12 point to White's 9 point, hitting Black's blot and putting him on the bar.

Black rolls 4 and 3.

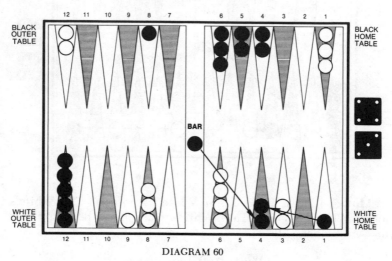

DIAGRAM 60

Enter White's board on White's 4 point and move the man on White's 1 point to White's 4 point. Black has made White's 4 point. In our first game, I mentioned that your own 4 point was the second most important point in your board—therefore, it must also be an important point for an opponent to make. Its value lies in the fact that it creates a block that will impede White's freedom of movement. This point also is a landing spot for any of Black's blots which may be hit in the future. These men have also moved to a position where large doubles will permit them to move more easily toward their destination.

68

White rolls double 5's.

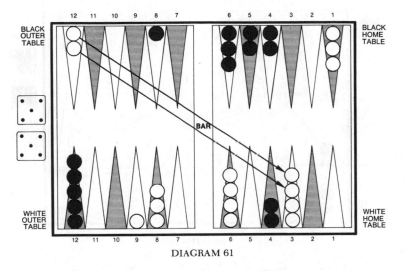

DIAGRAM 61

An unpleasant roll for White. Move two men from Black's 12 point to White's 3 point. An alternative play would have been to move two men from Black's 12 point to White's 8 point and two men from White's 6 point to White's 1 point. I prefer the former because it leaves White's men more evenly distributed.

69

Black rolls 6 and 1.

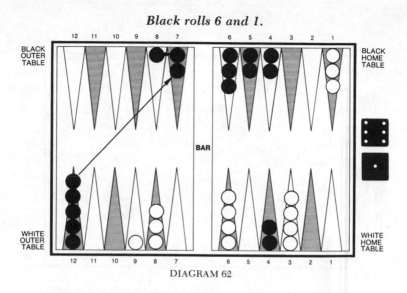

DIAGRAM 62

(I'll bet you know this move!) Make Black's bar point. Oh, boy—White's in trouble now! Your three men on Black's 1 point cannot move 3's, 4's, 5's, or 6's.

White rolls 6 and 5.

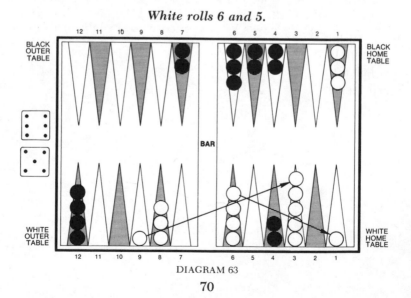

DIAGRAM 63

70

Move one man from White's 9 point to White's 3 point and one man from White's 6 point to White's 1 point. This was another terrible roll, one that left little choice in playing.

Black rolls double 5's.

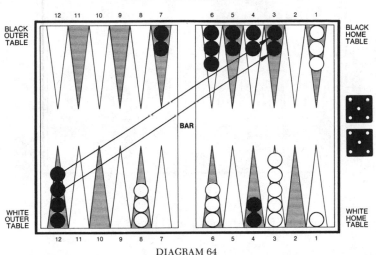

DIAGRAM 64

Move two men from White's 12 point to Black's 3 point. This is preferable to making Black's 8 point and moving two men from White's 4 point to White's 9 point. By making Black's 3 point, Black has created a block which is 5 points long, only one point short of a "prime." A *prime* is a block that is six contiguous points long, of the same color of men. Once a prime has been established, your opponent's man or men can't move past it until it has been broken, since all of the six numbers on the dice are blocked. As you can see, if Black makes either Black's 8 point or his 2 point, he will have made a prime. Black's men on White's 4 point will not have difficulty in moving out of White's board.

White rolls 6 and 4.

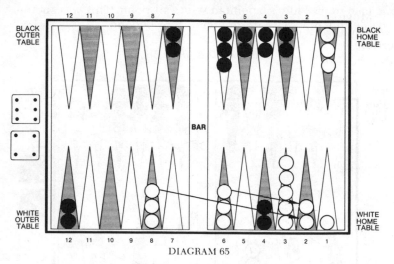

DIAGRAM 65

Make White's 2 point. Again, no choice.

Black rolls 4 and 2.

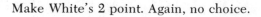
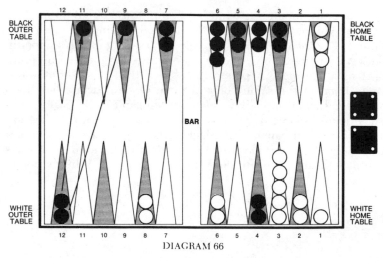

DIAGRAM 66

72

Move one man from White's 12 point to Black's 11 point and one man from White's 12 point to Black's 9 point.

In the event White rolls a 1 and 6 (the only number that will get one of the men out of Black's inner board), Black wants his men spread out so as to increase the chances of hitting White's resulting blot. Black's blots cannot be hit by White.

White rolls 6 and 5.

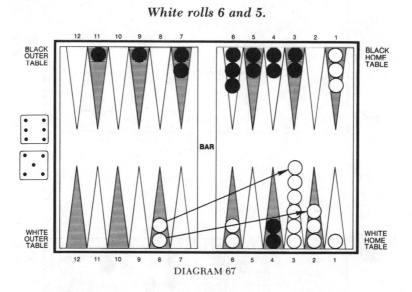

DIAGRAM 67

Move one man from White's 8 point to White's 3 point, and one man from White's 8 point to White's 2 point.

Black rolls 3 and 1.

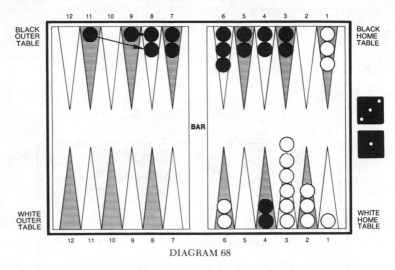

DIAGRAM 68

Make Black's 8 point (Black now has a prime).

White rolls 5 and 3.

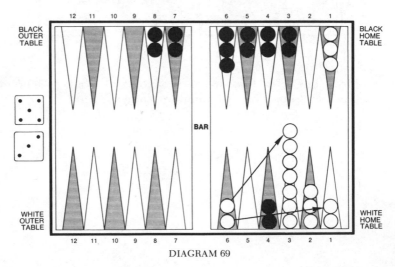

DIAGRAM 69

Move one man from White's 6 point to White's 3 point and one man from White's 6 point to White's 1 point. This is what is known as a "forced play." There is only one man that White can move 5 and only one man that will move 3. You now see why there was no rush to move Black's men on White's 4 point, since White had almost no choice as to movement in his last several rolls.

Black rolls double 6's.

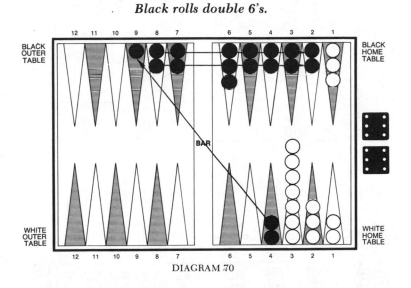

DIAGRAM 70

Make Black's 2 point—known as "advancing the prime"—and move one man from White's 4 point to Black's 9 point. The block is still six long, but it has moved forward. Beyond the prime it is not necessary to keep the men together, since White cannot hit them.

White rolls 4 and 2.

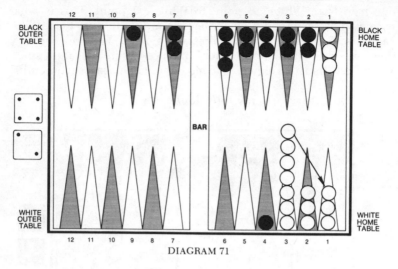

DIAGRAM 71

Move one man to White's 1 point from White's 3 point. White has no 4 to play.

Black rolls 4 and 5.

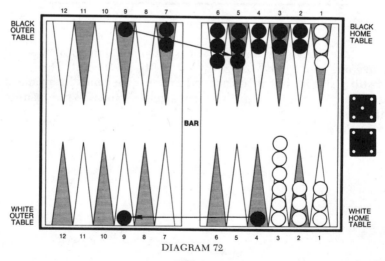

DIAGRAM 72

76

Move one man from White's 4 point to White's 9 point and one man from Black's 9 point to Black's 5 point.

In general, when you have a prime that ends at your bar and when your opponent has men on your 1 point, it is best to try to bring the additional men into your home board, on the higher points. (It requires only 12 men—two men on each of the 6 points—to have a prime. You will therefore have three additional men.)

White rolls double 4's

No moves!
(Remember, you may not bear off until all of your men are in your home board.)

Black rolls 6 and 5.

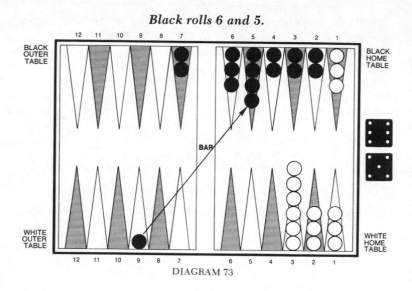

DIAGRAM 73

Move one man from White's 9 point to Black's 5 point. Black is still maintaining the prime, preventing White from moving out of Black's board.

White rolls 2 and 1.

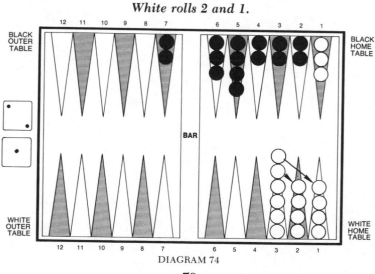

DIAGRAM 74

78

Move two men from White's 3 point, one to White's 2 point and one to White's 1 point.

Black rolls 5 and 3.

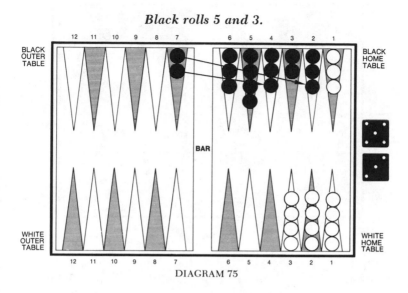

DIAGRAM 75

Move the men from Black's bar to Black's 4 point and Black's 2 point.

White rolls 6 and 3.

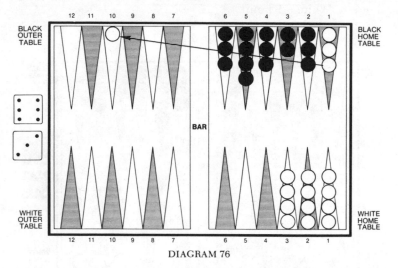

DIAGRAM 76

Since Black has at last broken his prime you now can move from his board. Move one man to Black's 10 point—a forced move.

Black rolls 6 and 5.

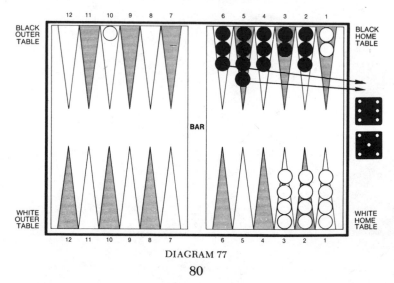

DIAGRAM 77

80

(Black can now commence bearing off.) Bear one man off Black's 6 point and one man off Black's 5 point.

White rolls 4 and 3.

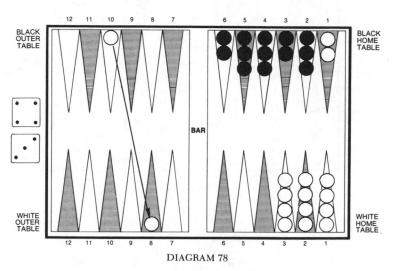

DIAGRAM 78

Again, a forced move. Move from Black's 10 point to White's 8 point.

Black rolls 5 and 1.

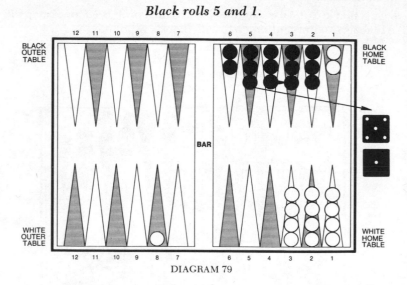

DIAGRAM 79

Bear one man off Black's 5 point and move one man from Black's 4 point to Black's 3 point.

White rolls 5 and 4.

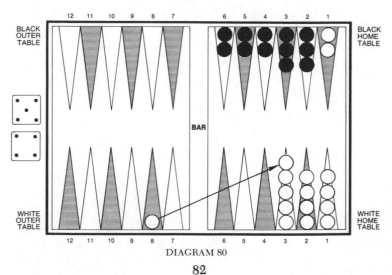

DIAGRAM 80

Move one man 5 from White's 8 point to White's 3 point. You have no 4 to play (when it is possible to play either, but not both, numbers of your roll, then you must play the *larger* of the two numbers, if possible).

Black rolls double 6's.

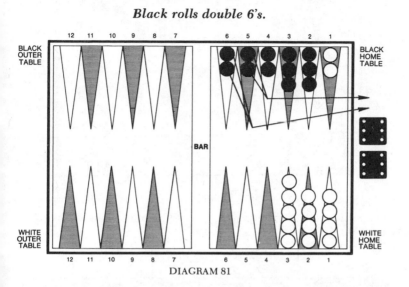

DIAGRAM 81

Bear four men off—two from Black's 6 point and two from Black's 5 point.

83

White rolls 5 and 3.

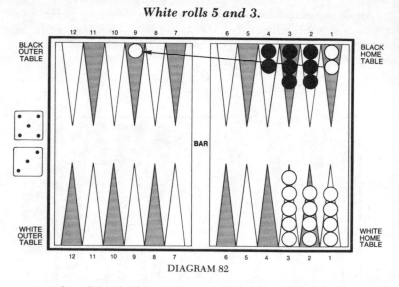

DIAGRAM 82

Another forced play. Move one man from Black's 1 point to Black's 9 point.

Black rolls 6 and 4.

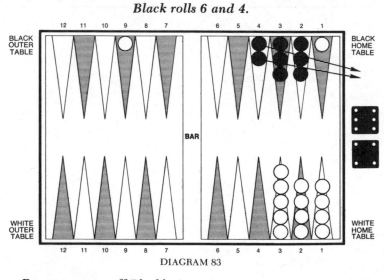

DIAGRAM 83

Bear two men off Black's 4 point.

84

White rolls double 2's.

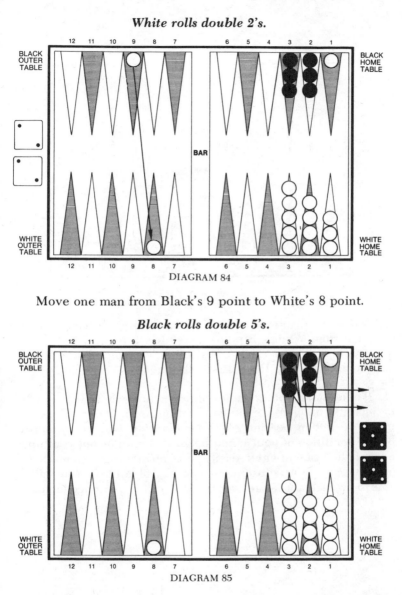

DIAGRAM 84

Move one man from Black's 9 point to White's 8 point.

Black rolls double 5's.

DIAGRAM 85

Bear three men off Black's 3 point and one man from Black's 2 point.

85

White rolls 6 and 2.

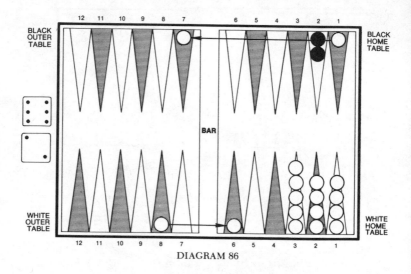

DIAGRAM 86

Move one man from Black's 1 point to Black's bar point, and one man from White's 8 point to White's 6 point. By removing the man from Black's inner board you have avoided being "backgammoned"—losing three times the amount you were playing for.

There will be other games of this nature where you may risk being backgammoned in hopes of hitting an opponent's blot which might be left in bearing off. Your decision will be influenced by the condition of your home board (whether or not your opponent, if hit, can re-enter easily), his chances of leaving a blot or blots, and your subsequent chances of hitting. You will be able to evaluate this more accurately as your experience increases.

86

Black rolls 3 and 2.

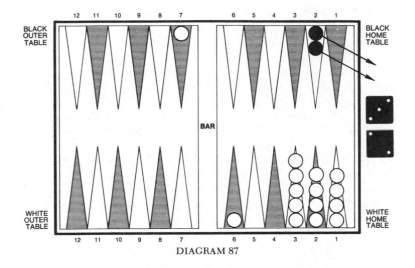

DIAGRAM 87

Bear off Black's last two men, winning a "gammon" (twice the amount of the stake being played for).

If in this second game, you made some of the moves before looking at my directions—great! It shows you're getting the knack of it after only two games. I'm impressed.

Let's take a moment for a short résumé of some of the more important material that has been covered. You have discovered that at the start of a game the making of points in your home board is of the utmost importance. You have learned that these points are important because they

1) create an effective block against any opposition men in your home board;
2) create a safe landing spot for your men;
3) make re-entry to your home board more difficult for your opponent.

You have been shown that an inability to move your men out of your opponent's home board can be disastrous. (Refer back to your three men on Black's 1 point in Game Two.) Therefore, while it is very important to make points in your outer and home boards, it is imperative that you start moving your men from your

87

opponent's 1 point early in the game, before he can create blocks that will prevent them from moving.

Before starting Game Three, I want to discuss responses to opening moves. These are the moves you will make after your opponent has won the opening roll. Any attempt to cover all of the possible moves that could be made after an opponent's opening roll would require a book in itself. There are fifteen actual opening rolls, many of which can be played in several ways. There are twenty-one possible numbers that can be rolled—the fifteen we have discussed, plus six possible doubles. If one took every combination of the conceivable positions after the first two rolls, the figure would be in the thousands.

There are a few moves you should know. Most of these are concerned with doubles. As for the remainder, what I mentioned before about "anticipating future moves" will help you in making your decisions as to what is the correct move in a given circumstance.

Anticipating future moves means *trying to see ahead.* For example, "What am I trying to accomplish and how do I go about it?" "What will happen if I make this or that move?" "What will the position look like if my opponent makes this point or that point?" "Now that my opponent has made his bar point, what will occur if I don't start my two men on his 1 point moving forward?" "Will I be trapped?" And so on. Each roll will change the questions you must ask yourself. If you can anticipate what is likely to happen, you may often be able to make a move that will be advantageous.

Let's pause and look at a few plays that should be more or less automatic. Then I'll show you how "anticipation" works.

Black's first roll 6 and 5; White rolls double 1's

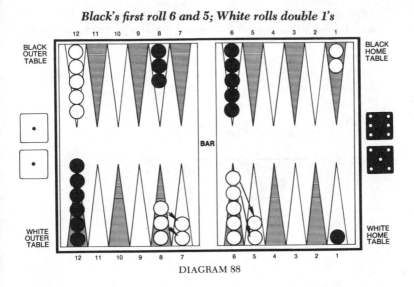

DIAGRAM 88

Make your bar and your 5 point—unless your opponent has split the two men that started on your 1 point. (By that, I mean: when he has a man on the 1 point but his other man has moved to your 2, 3, or 4 point.)

Black's first roll 6 and 5; White rolls double 2's

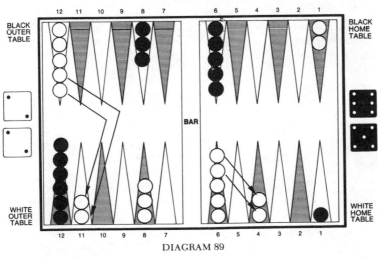

DIAGRAM 89

After an opponent's opening roll of 6 and 5, 3 and 1, 4 and 2, or 6 and 1. (We *know* how the opponent will play these numbers.) Make your 4 point and your 11 point. All other plays are so dependent on what your opponent did on his opening roll that the answers will fall under the explanation of how to play your numbers in "anticipation of future moves."

Black's first roll 6 and 5; White rolls double 3's

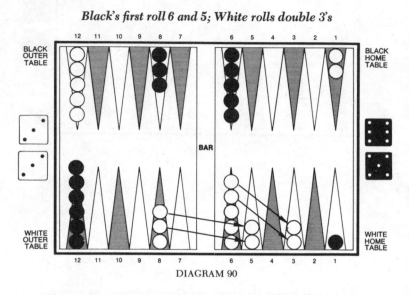

DIAGRAM 90

When your opponent has rolled 5 and 2, 6 and 5, or 5 and 4, make 2 points in your inner board. The other plays will vary as with double 2's.

90

Black's first roll 6 and 5; White rolls double 4's

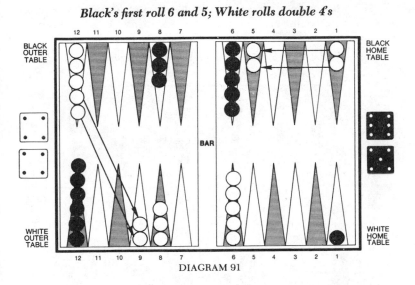

DIAGRAM 91

If your opponent has rolled 6 and 5, 6 and 1, 4 and 2, make his 5 point and your 9 point. As with the other doubles many varied plays can be made; they will change according to your opponent's opening roll.

Black's first roll 4 and 2; White rolls double 5's

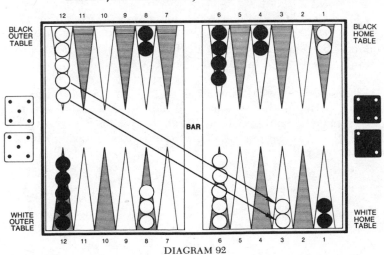

DIAGRAM 92

If your opponent has not split his two men on your 1 point, make your 3 point by moving two men from Black's 12 point.

Black's first roll 6 and 5; White rolls double 6's

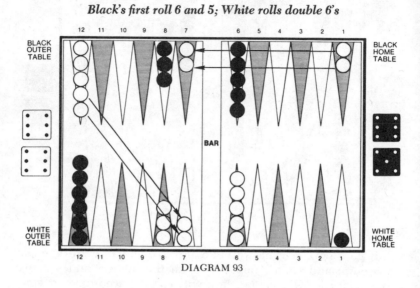

DIAGRAM 93

Unless your opponent started with 6 and 1, make his bar and your bar. If he *did* start with 6 and 1, make your bar and your 2 point.

With double 3's, 4's, and 5's, whenever it is possible to hit an opponent's blot in your home board, you should make two points. The 5 and 3 points with double 3's, the 4 and 2 points with double 4's, and the 3 and 1 points with double 5's.

Let's now see what I meant by "how your move is influenced by anticipating"—that is, what will happen as a result of certain moves made by your opponent. To do this we are going to assume Black wins the opening roll. Then you try to see what we should do with our roll.

Black starts with 2 and 1.

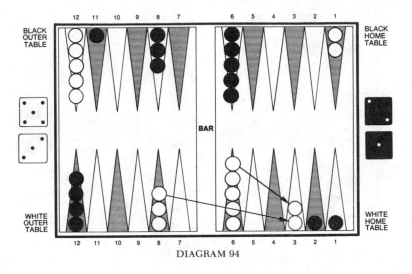

DIAGRAM 94

1) You now roll 5 and 3. Make your 3 point.

The alternate play of moving two men from Black's 12 point to White's 10 and 8 points would expose your blot on the 10 point to two men, since Black has split his men in your home board.

93

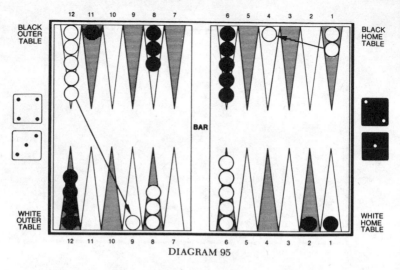

DIAGRAM 95

2) Your roll is 4 and 3. Move one man to Black's 4 point and one man from Black's 12 point to White's 9 point.

We do *not* move to Black's 5 point, "anticipating" that the probabilities of Black's making his 5 point have increased due to the extra man on Black's 11 point.

In general it is best to avoid bringing a blot to a space where the opponent has several men directly bearing—a direct shot—on it. ("Directly bearing" means 6 pips or less away.)

94

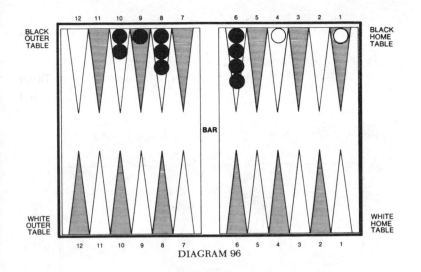

DIAGRAM 96

(Example 1) All of Black's men in his outer and home board are said to be directly bearing on White's blot on Black's 4 point.

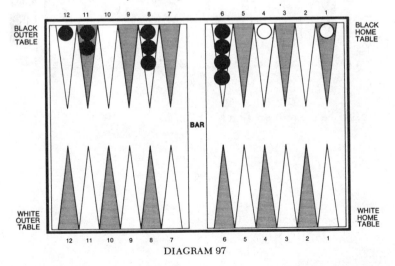

DIAGRAM 97

(Example 2) Now only the men on Black's 6 point and 8 point are directly bearing on White's blot. Black's men on Black's 11

and 12 points are more than 6 pips away from White's blot on Black's 4 point. Therefore they are not directly bearing on this blot.

In Diagram 96, White must avoid putting a blot within direct range of all these men because he should anticipate being "pointed on" by Black.

Black's first roll 2 and 1; White rolls 6 and 4

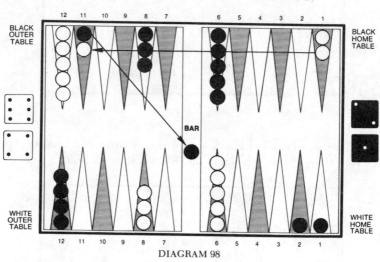

DIAGRAM 98

Hit Black's blot on Black's 11 point.

Black's first roll 2 and 1; White rolls double 4's

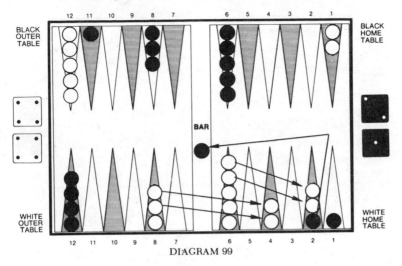

DIAGRAM 99

Make the 4 point and the 2 point in your inner board. (As I pointed out before, whenever it is possible to hit an opponent's blot and make two points in your home board on your first roll, this play should be made.)

White rolls 4 and 2, 3 and 1, 6 and 1, or 6 and 5: These rolls are treated as though they were opening rolls.

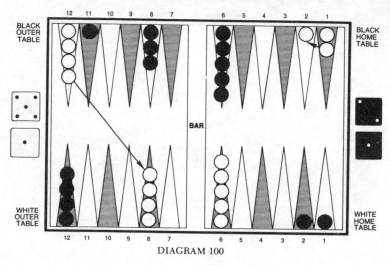

DIAGRAM 100

Move one man from Black's 12 point to your 8 point and one man from Black's 1 point to Black's 2 point.

We anticipate that Black has a good chance to make either his bar point or his 5 point on his next roll due to the increased chances that his blot on his 11 point affords him. Therefore, you must start moving your men in his home board, before they become blocked. By splitting these men, you also increase your chances of hitting any blot which Black may have in his outer or home board.

Black starts with 6 and 5. Treat all of White's rolls as opening rolls.

98

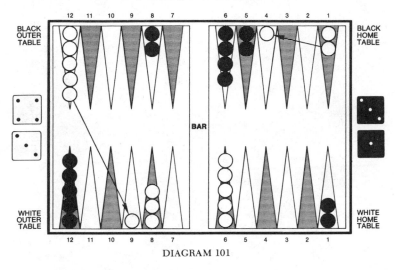

DIAGRAM 101

1) White rolls 4 and 3.

Move one man to Black's 4 point and one man from Black's 12 point to your 9 point.

In anticipation of a subsequent good roll by Black, which would block your men on Black's 1 point from movement, you must attempt to establish a more advanced point in Black's board, or you must escape entirely the block which he has started to build.

99

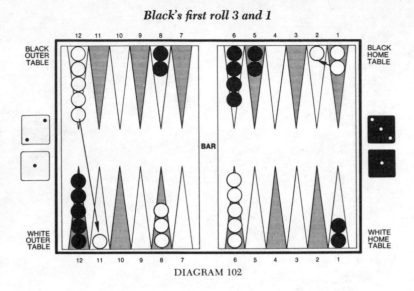

DIAGRAM 102

2) White rolls 2 and 1.

Move one man from Black's 1 to Black's 2 point, and one man from Black's 12 to White's 11 points—again, the necessity of attempting to avoid being trapped on Black's 1 point and at the same time bringing builders which will help make valuable points of your own.

3) White rolls 3 and 1, 4 and 2, 6 and 1, 6 and 5, or 5 and 3. All played if an opening roll.

Black's first roll 3 and 1

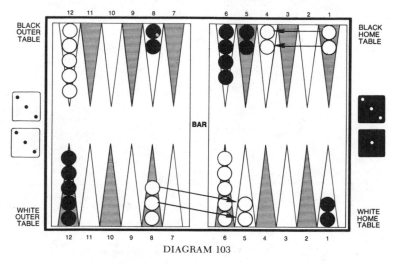

DIAGRAM 103

4) White rolls double 3's.

Make Black's 4 point and either your 5 point, 3 point, or bring two men from Black's 12 point to your 10 point. The important move in this case is the move to Black's 4 point. Having this point prevents you from being blocked from movement out of Black's home board. You also create a block against Black's freedom of movement in Black's outer board. The other two 3's may be played in any one of three ways. Which you choose will depend on your style of play—aggressive or conservative.

I am not going to devote any more time to this phase of backgammon—the responses to opening rolls. I feel that you will learn from experience much more quickly than by reading each of the thousands of possibilities. Almost always the correct play will be made if you answer the questions I listed earlier when I discussed anticipation.

White rolls 4 and Black rolls 2.

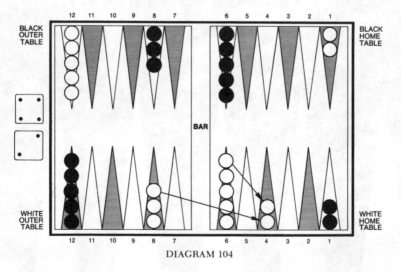

DIAGRAM 104

Make White's 4 point (one of the automatic opening moves).

104

Black rolls 5 and 1.

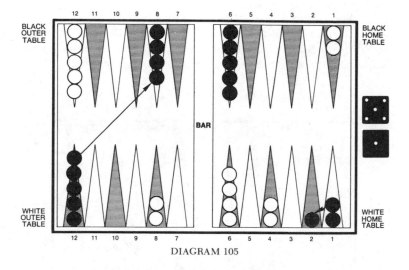

DIAGRAM 105

Move one man from White's 12 point to Black's 8 point and move one man from White's 1 point to White's 2 point.

It is important for several reasons that Black start his back men, the two men that start on an opponent's 1 point. White has started blocking Black's movement because White has made his 4 point. If, on White's next roll, he is fortunate enough to make his bar, 5, 3, or 2 point, then Black's road to escape will be most difficult. If it is possible to make an advanced point in your opponent's home board you should do so. By splitting your back men you increase your chances of doing this. When your men are together, to move to any advanced point in one roll requires doubles. In this case, if Black's men had remained together on White's 1 point, in order to make a more advanced point (the 2, 3, 4, or bar) Black would have to roll either double 1's, 2's, 4's, or 6's. This occurs only 4 times out of 36. When the back men are split on the 1 and 2 point, Black can make a more advanced point by rolling any 1 that will make the 2 point: double 1's, or 2 and 1, which will make the 3 point; 4 and 3, which will make the 5 point, or 6 and 5, which will make White's bar point. These possibilities will occur 15 times out of 36. (To check this, use the "Possible Combinations Chart" on page 49. By splitting,

105

your chances of making a more advanced point are almost four times greater than by not splitting.

Along with advantages of splitting there are some disadvantages. The fact that Black now has two blots will make it possible for White to hit these men or make a point on them. The risk that is taken is minor compared to the possible gain.

White rolls 4 and 5.

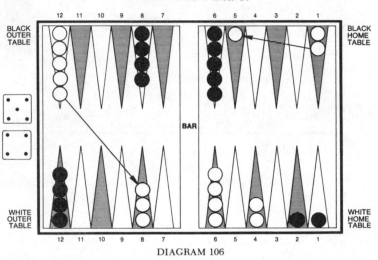

DIAGRAM 106

Move one man from Black's 1 point to Black's 5 point and one man from Black's 12 point to White's 8 point.

White needs a builder on his 8 point. This builder will enable White to make the bar point, 5 point, or 3 or 2 point, and still maintain the 8 point. The move to Black's 5 point is an attempt to make a more advanced point or to get to safety. You did not bring the four to White's 9 point from Black's 12 point because this blot is now exposed to two of Black's men, rather than one, which would have been the case if Black had not split his back men.

Black rolls 2 and 1.

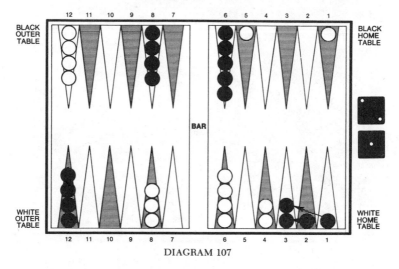

DIAGRAM 107

Make White's 3 point.

One of the basic objectives is to make advanced points in the opponent's board. Black now has a safe landing place and has made a point, which White will find annoying when the time comes for him to move his men into his home board.

White rolls 3 and 1.

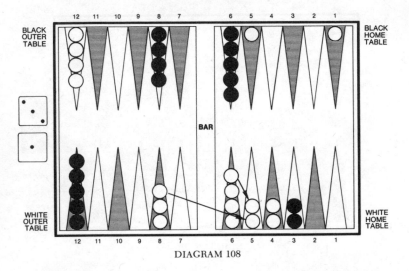

DIAGRAM 108

Make White's 5 point. You now see the importance of the builder. It would have been impossible to make the 5 point without leaving a blot on the 8 point.

White's board is now formidable and his position will allow Black to escape with 4's and 6's only. The alternative play would have been to make Black's 5 point. Since Black's board is not threatening (he has only one point and no builders on the 9, 10, or 11 point), there is nothing imperative about having to make this point.

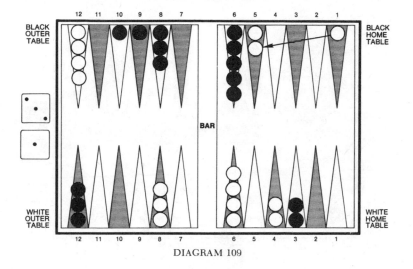

DIAGRAM 109

Take this position: the correct play would be to make Black's 5 point, since you would anticipate Black making his 5 point or his bar point, due to the extra men that are directly bearing on these points.

Black rolls 6 and 1.

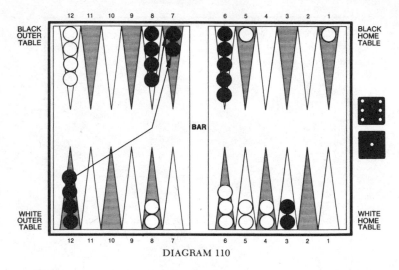

DIAGRAM 110

Make Black's bar point. Black is making an attempt to block White's men from moving out of Black's home board.

White rolls double 6's.

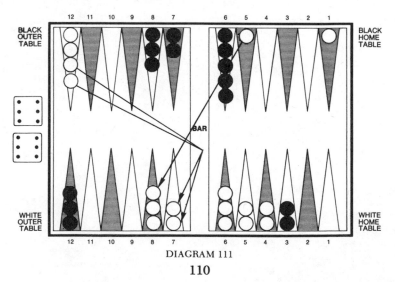

DIAGRAM 111

Make White's bar point, and move one man from Black's 5 point to White's 8 point. It is a good thing you moved to Black's 5 point previously; otherwise, two of your men would have been stuck on Black's 1 point instead of only one. White's block is now 5 long. Black can now escape with 6's only. White's biggest concern now is his blot on Black's 1 point.

Black rolls 4 and 2.

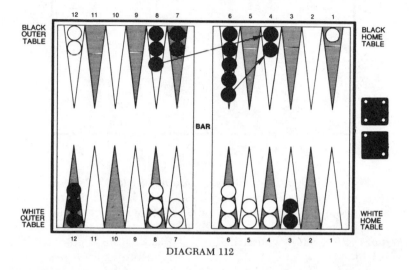

DIAGRAM 112

Make Black's 4 point, again attempting to prevent White's escaping.

White rolls 6 and 4.

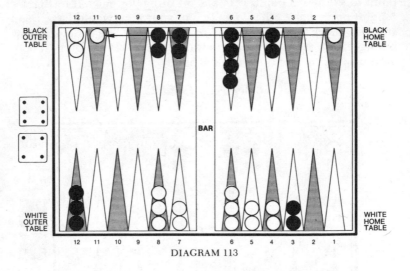

DIAGRAM 113

Move the man from Black's 1 point to Black's 11 point, and keep your fingers crossed that Black does not roll a 2 or an 11.

The opportunity to escape with this blot may not come again. We must try to bring him to safety. If you look back at the possible combinations chart you will see that Black will roll a 2 11 times on the average, out of 36, and 6 and 5 (hitting from White's 3 point) twice. The total of 13 out of 36 makes White a little less than a two-to-one favorite not to be hit.

Black rolls double 3's.

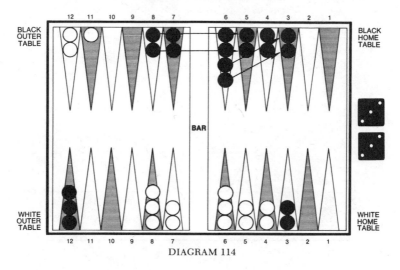

DIAGRAM 114

(Whew! He missed us.)

Make Black's 5 point and Black's 3 point. It looks as though we will get out of Black's home board just in time. Black must now hope to hit a blot of White's. White on the other hand must avoid leaving any blots that could be hit by Black.

113

White rolls 6 and 1.

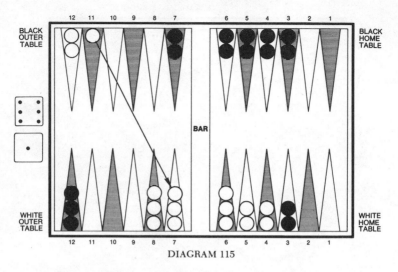

DIAGRAM 115

Not much to this play. Move White's blot on Black's 11 point to White's bar point.

Black rolls 6 and 2.

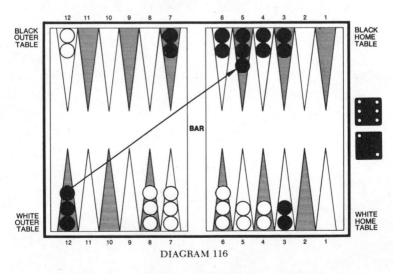

DIAGRAM 116

Bring one man from White's 12 point to Black's 5 point.

114

White rolls 6 and 5.

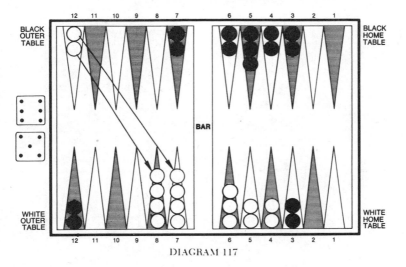

DIAGRAM 117

(Such a lovely roll!) Move one man to White's 8 point and one man to White's bar from Black's 12 point. This is done in preference to making the 2 point or 1 point, since this roll enables us to accomplish our objective of getting these two men to safety without leaving a blot that Black could hit.

115

Black rolls 5 and 3.

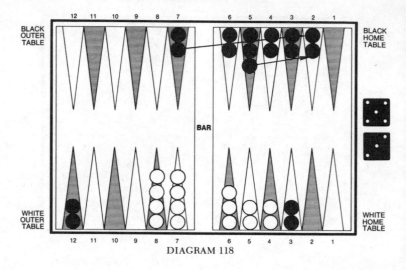

DIAGRAM 118

Make Black's 2 point. At this time Black is too far behind to be concerned with moving his men from board to board with the least number of wasted pips. His last hope is that White will have some difficulty in bringing his men into his home board and be forced to leave a blot, which Black might hit. One other very small chance for Black is to roll several large doubles while White is rolling small numbers, and, as a result, be able to beat White in the race.

White rolls 6 and 5.

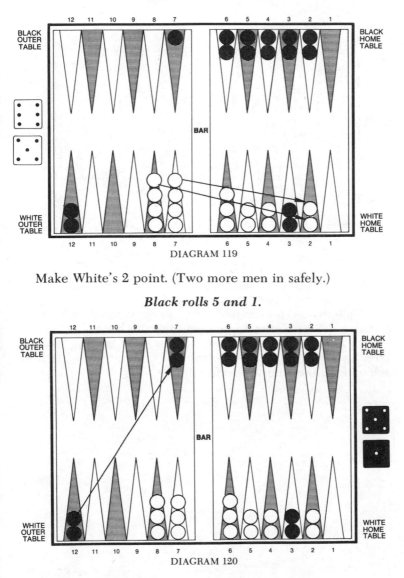

DIAGRAM 119

Make White's 2 point. (Two more men in safely.)

Black rolls 5 and 1.

DIAGRAM 120

Make Black's bar. Nothing is better, and, if Black does hit a blot of White's, Black will have a prime—and therefore a difficult barrier for White's newly starting man to overcome.

White rolls double 5's.

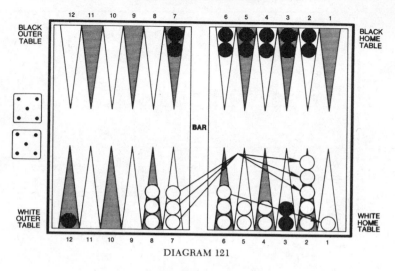

DIAGRAM 121

Move three men from White's bar to White's 2 point and one man from the 6 point to the 1 point.

An alternative play would be to move three men from the 6 point to the 1 point and one man from the bar to the 2 point. In doing this, however, you would lose a good landing spot (the 6 point), and this will make it even more difficult for you to bring the men from the outer board in safely.

Black rolls 5 and 2.

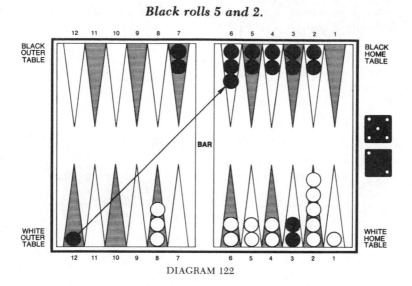

DIAGRAM 122

Move one man to Black's 6 point from White's 12 point. Black still maintains his prime, which appears to be more and more ominous to White, since he is finding Black's block on his 3 point quite annoying.

White rolls 6 and 4.

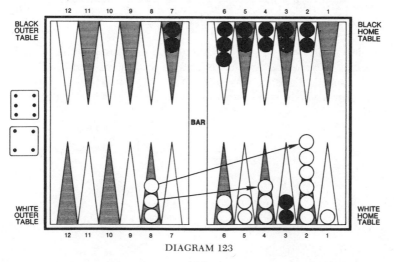

DIAGRAM 123

119

Move one man from the 8 point to the 4 point and one man from the 8 point to the 2 point. The 6 was forced, and, although you could have moved a 4 from the 6 or 5 point, you still would have left a blot. If the blot were missed you would then still have the problem of getting the men in from the 8 point. Now, at least, if your blot is missed it will not be difficult to bring that man into your home board.

Black rolls 5 and 2.

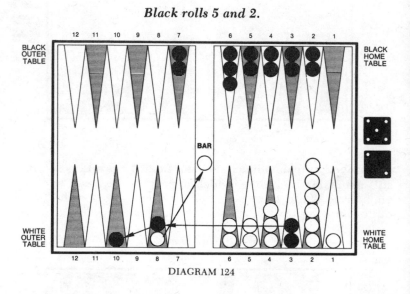

DIAGRAM 124

Hit White's blot on the 8 point and continue to the 10 point. Black is now rewarded for his careful play in maintaining his home board. True, it was most unlucky for White to have left a blot, but since he did Black must be in a position to take advantage of it.

White rolls 1 and 6.

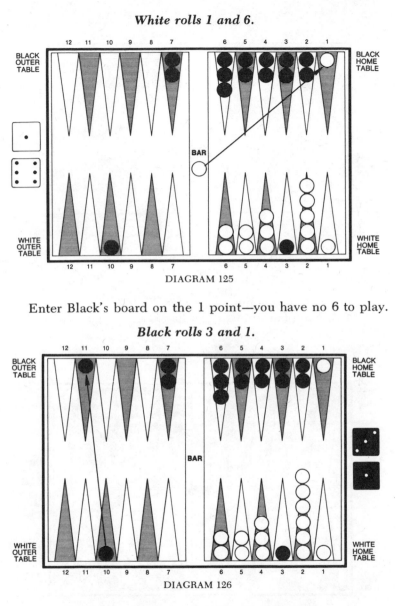

DIAGRAM 125

Enter Black's board on the 1 point—you have no 6 to play.

Black rolls 3 and 1.

DIAGRAM 126

Move from White's 10 point to Black's 11 point.

121

White rolls 6 and 5.

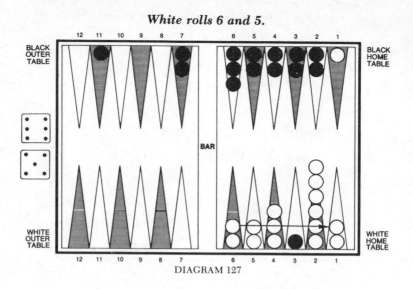

DIAGRAM 127

(The situation is getting worse for White.)

Only a 5 to play and that is a forced move from the 6 point to the 1 point.

Black rolls double 5's.

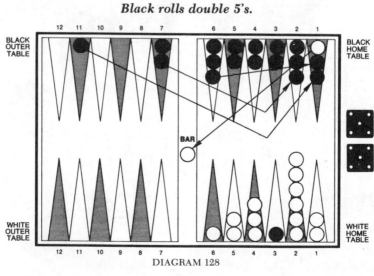

DIAGRAM 128

Close Black's home board by moving one man from Black's 11 point to the 1 point and one man from the 6 point to the 1 point. Move the last 5 from the bar to the 2 point.

Black left his man on White's 3 point in hopes that he will roll a 3 and pick up White's blot on the 6 point. If this occurs Black will have a chance to win a gammon from White. The only risk he takes by not moving the man from White's 3 point is that if on his next roll he rolls double 2's, he will be forced to break his board. The odds against this are 35 to 1. This is not much of a risk to take when you consider the possible gain.

White cannot roll.

Black rolls 3 and 1.

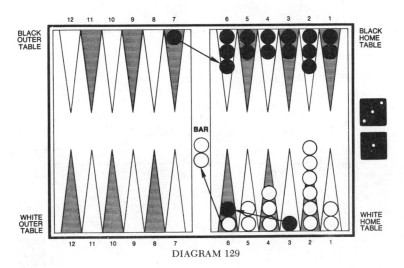

DIAGRAM 129

Hit White's blot on White's 6 point and move one man from Black's bar to Black's 6 point. Again Black's careful play has been rewarded.

White cannot move.

123

Black rolls 6 and 4.

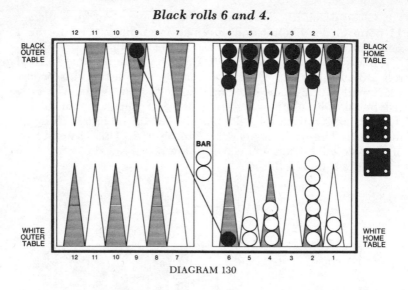

DIAGRAM 130

Move from White's 6 point to Black's 9 point.
White cannot roll.

Black rolls 5 and 4.

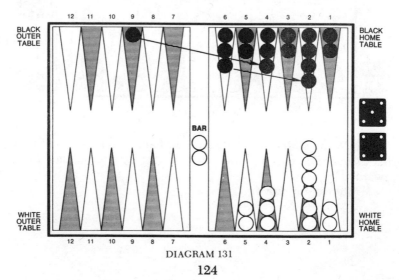

DIAGRAM 131

124

Move the man from Black's 9 point 5 to Black's 4 point, and one man 4 from Black's 6 point to Black's 2 point.

If Black were to bring the man from his 9 point to his 5 point and then bear him off, the position would be such that a subsequent roll of double 6's, double 5's, 6 and 5, 6 and 4, or 6 and 3 would cause Black to leave a blot:

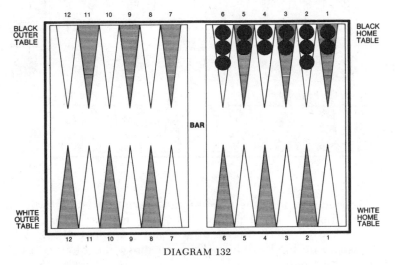

DIAGRAM 132

With the play Black chose, no number will cause a blot. White can't roll.

Black rolls 6 and 2.

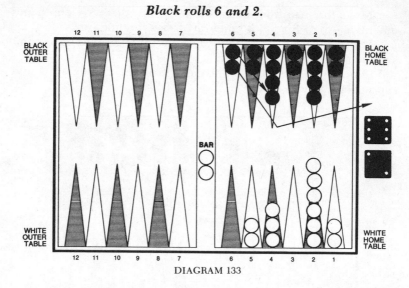

DIAGRAM 133

Bear one man off the 6 point and move the remaining man on the 6 point to the 4 point. Had White not had men on the bar, Black would have borne off a 6 and a 2. Since Black does not wish to be hit by White, he must move the blot on the 6 point to the 4 point.

White rolls double 5's.

He cannot enter—therefore, no moves.

Black rolls 6 and 4.

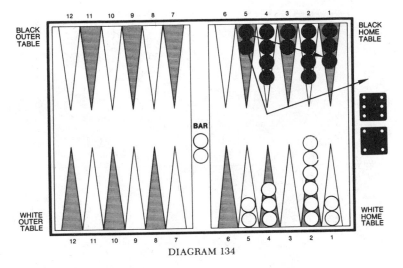

DIAGRAM 134

Bear one man off the 5 point (considering the 6 as a 5, since there are no 6's to be moved) and move one man from the 5 point to the 1 point—again not giving White a chance to hit a blot on the 5 point, which would have been exposed if Black had taken a man off the 4 point with the 4.

White rolls 6 and 3.

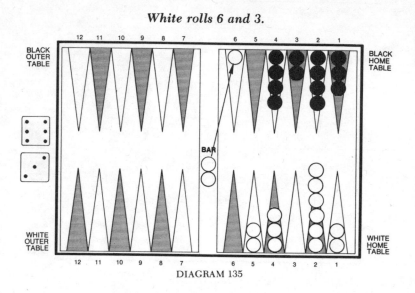

DIAGRAM 135

Enter one man on Black's 6 point. The remaining man cannot enter. (Remember, you can't move if one or more of your men are on the bar.)

Black rolls double 4's.

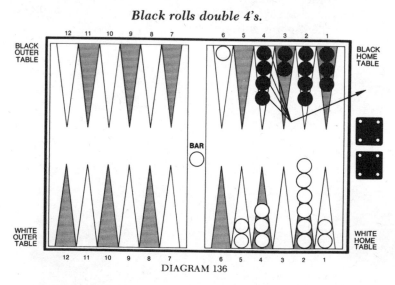

DIAGRAM 136

Bear four men from the 4 point.

128

White rolls 4 and 1.

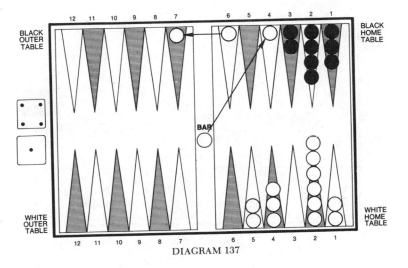

DIAGRAM 137

Enter on Black's 4 point and move one man from Black's 6 point to Black's bar. (You are using the knowledge that you should try to move from board to board with the least number of wasted pips when you are attempting to move as quickly as possible.)

Black rolls 5 and 1.

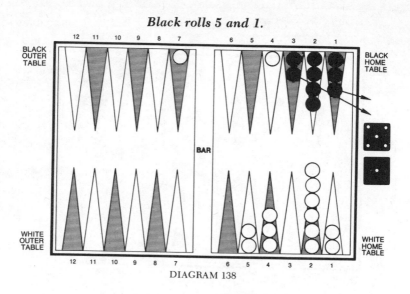

DIAGRAM 138

Bear one man off the 3 point and one man from the 1 point. Now that White's men are no longer in a position to hit Black, Black bears off without fear of leaving a blot.

White rolls 6 and 4.

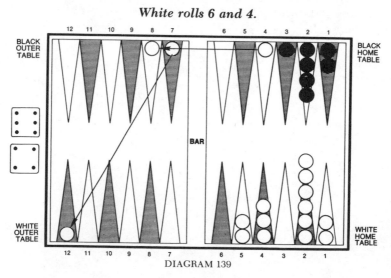

DIAGRAM 139

130

Move 6 from Black's bar to White's 12 point and 4 from Black's 4 point to Black's 8 point.

Black rolls 5 and 4.

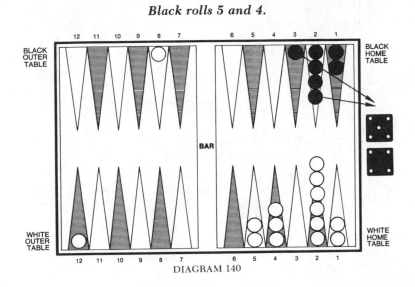

DIAGRAM 140

Bear one man off the 3 point and one man from the 2 point.

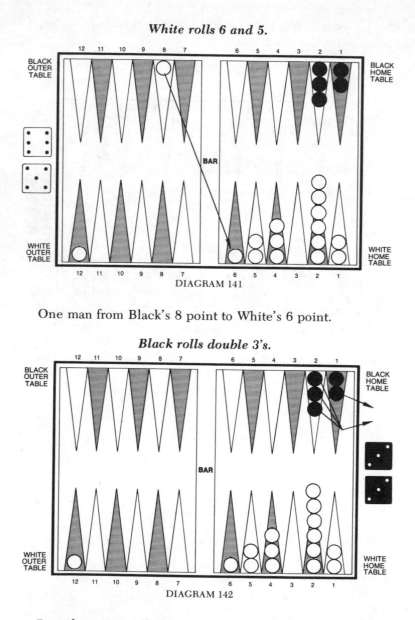

White rolls 6 and 5.

DIAGRAM 141

One man from Black's 8 point to White's 6 point.

Black rolls double 3's.

DIAGRAM 142

Bear three men off Black's 2 point and one man from Black's 1 point.

White rolls double 2's.

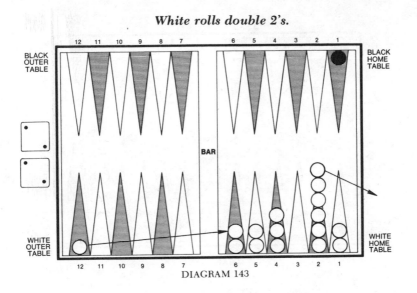

DIAGRAM 143

Move one man from White's 12 point to White's 6 point and bear one man off the 2 point. That was close: You barely saved a gammon. Just to show the importance of not wasting pips—when running, put White's man, which was on White's 12 point, back 1 pip to Black's 12 point.

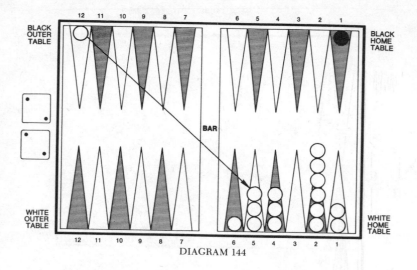

DIAGRAM 144

Now, double 2's would not bear a man off for White.

All I can say for this game is that you were unlucky to lose it, but very lucky to save a gammon. This is not much of a consolation, but it is better than nothing.

Well, how do you like backgammon?

I hope you find it fascinating. It is!

Every game of backgammon that you will play will be considered either a "running game," a "blocking game," or a "back game." As we have discovered, our objective at the start of every game is a combination of both running and blocking. We are racing to get our men into our home board, and at the same time attempting to block, by establishing points, the movement of our opponent's men.

134

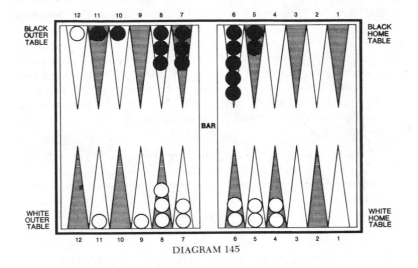

DIAGRAM 145

When all your men have passed all of your opponent's men (a game in which no further contact, or hitting, is possible), the game is termed a straight "running game." The back game is by far the most difficult to master. Very few backgammon players play the back game really well. Fortunately, it is a type of game that you won't have to play often, and one that all players should avoid if possible. The fact that one should avoid the back game does not preclude the importance of having a working understanding of why it is played and how it works. Unfortunately, it is neither possible nor practical now to cover this phase of backgammon in depth; your experience is too limited. Once you have absorbed the basics, which will be quite simple, and have played several games, you may find the intricacies of the back game totally intriguing.

Now, let's see what conditions could force a player to attempt to play a back game.

When your opponent has had a series of large rolls, and one or more of your men, other than those that start on your opponent's 1 point, have been hit, you will find yourself hopelessly behind in a running game. It is at this juncture that you must change tactics.

In a running game your objective is to move forward as rapidly as possible; the reverse is true of the back game. As a matter

135

of fact you will attempt to do almost everything in reverse of what you have learned is correct for the running and blocking game. Instead of blocking your opponent's forward movement, you will try to facilitate it. Instead of avoiding blots, leave them. Instead of attempting to make advanced points in your opponent's home board, attempt to make low points. In the broadest of concepts, your objective is to *retreat* rather than advance! You must go slowly and your opponent must go rapidly. Here are some prerequisites to a successful back game:

1) You must have 2 points in your opponent's home board. (The lower the point the better. The 1 and 2 or 1 and 3 are the best. The 2 and 3 or 1 and 4 are good but not quite as effective. The 2 and 4, 3 and 4, 3 and 5, and 4 and 5 are a little less desirable, and the 1 and 5 are the least effective.)

2) Your own home board should not be too advanced. By this I mean that when you start to go into the back game you should not have already made your 1 or 2 point. When the time comes for your opponent to start bearing off, the high points in your home board should be closed. If all of your men are on your low points when you hit an opponent's blot, that blot will merely re-enter and proceed unmolested back to his home board.

3) Your opponent must be well ahead of you in the race. (He has rolled high numbers and you have rolled small numbers.)

When these conditions exist, without exception, your chances of playing and winning a back game are excellent.

Now, it is time to move on to Game Four.

136

White rolls 5 and Black rolls 4.

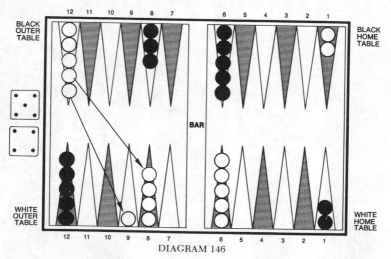

DIAGRAM 146

Move one man to White's 9 point and one man to White's 8 point from Black's 12 point.

138

Black rolls 6 and 2.

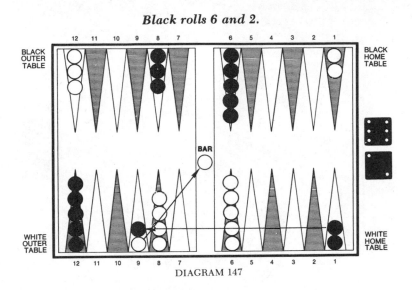

DIAGRAM 147

Hit White's blot on White's 9 point.

White rolls 2 and 4.

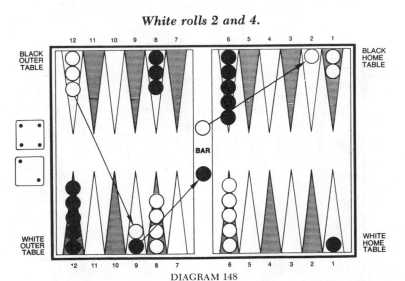

DIAGRAM 148

Enter on Black's two point and hit Black's blot on White's 9 point.

139

Black rolls 6 and 3.

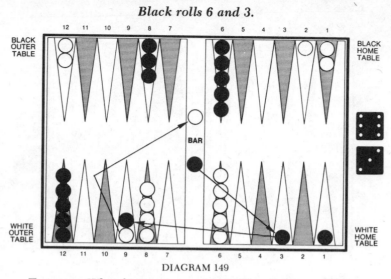

DIAGRAM 149

Enter on White's 3 point and hit White's blot on White's 9 point.

White rolls double 6's—and cannot enter.

Black rolls double 5's.

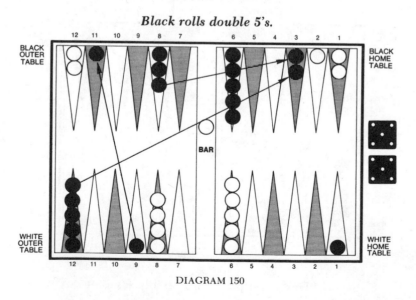

DIAGRAM 150

Move one man from White's 12 point to Black's 3 point, one

140

man from Black's 8 point to Black's 3 point, and one man from White's 9 point to Black's 11 point.

White rolls 2 and 1

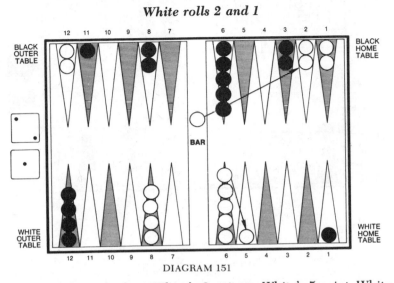

DIAGRAM 151

Move one man from White's 6 point to White's 5 point. White must now attempt to play a back game, since all of the conditions that are necessary are present.

1) White has two points in Black's home board.
2) As a result of being hit and due to Black's large rolls, White is well behind in the race.
3) White's remaining men (those not in Black's home board) have not advanced too far.

White dropped a blot on his 5 point because he is hoping to force Black to hit his blots (the opposite of the running game). This will achieve the desired result of slowing down forward movement.

Black rolls 6 and 1.

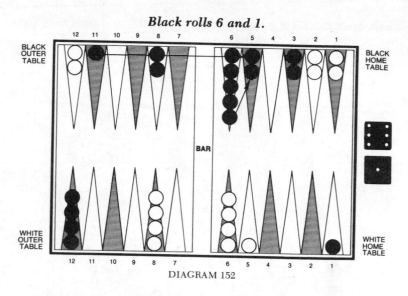

DIAGRAM 152

Make Black's 5 point.

White rolls 5 and 2.

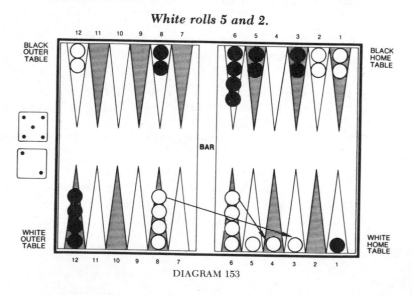

DIAGRAM 153

Move one man from White's 8 point to White's 3 point and

142

one man from White's 6 point to White's 4 point. (Again, White is hoping to force Black to hit him.)

Black rolls double 6's.

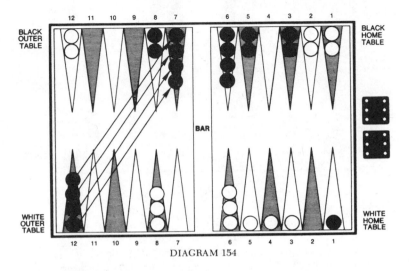

DIAGRAM 154

Move four men from White's 12 point to Black's bar point.

White rolls 6 and 1.

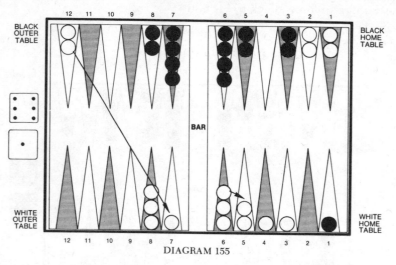

DIAGRAM 155

Move one man from Black's 12 point to White's bar and one man from White's 6 point to White's 5 point.

White made the 5 point rather than the bar because he is not trying to block Black's movement from White's home board. White could have left a blot on the 5 point by moving the man from Black's 12 point to White's 12 point. But, since he has enough blots for Black to hit, the 5 point must eventually be made, and he might as well do it now.

Black rolls double 6's.

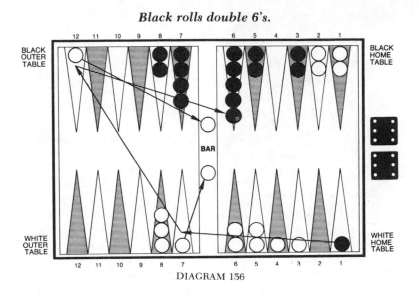

DIAGRAM 156

(This is a forced move.) Move one man from White's 1 point to Black's 6 point, hitting White's blot on White's bar and White's blot on Black's 12 point.

Black has only three 6's he can play.

145

White rolls 2 and 6.

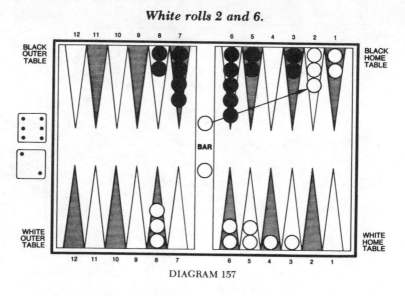

DIAGRAM 157

Enter one man on Black's 2 point.

Black rolls 5 and 3.

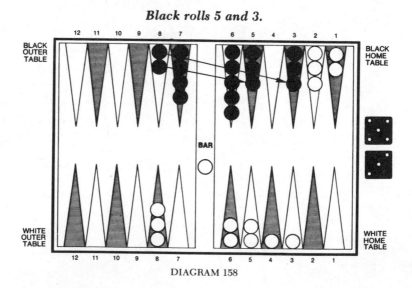

DIAGRAM 158

Move one man to Black's 5 point and one man to Black's 3 point from Black's 8 point.

146

White rolls 4 and 5.

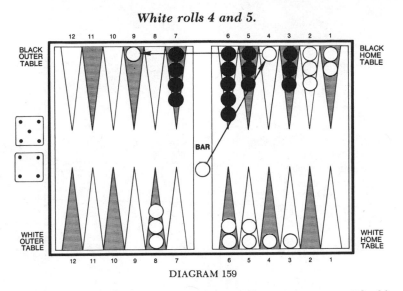

DIAGRAM 159

Enter on Black's 4 point and move the same man to Black's 9 point. Five men are enough to have in Black's board. Your objective now is to make the high points in your home board.

Black rolls 3 and 2.

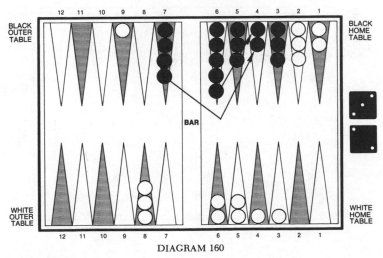

DIAGRAM 160

Make Black's 4 point.

147

White rolls 4 and 3.

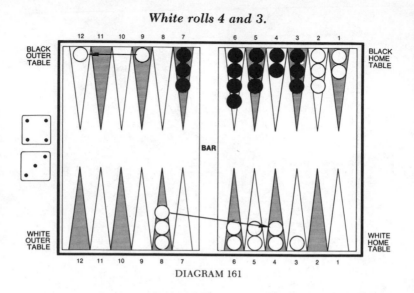

DIAGRAM 161

Make White's 4 point and move one man 3 from Black's 9 point to Black's 12 point.

Black rolls double 2's.

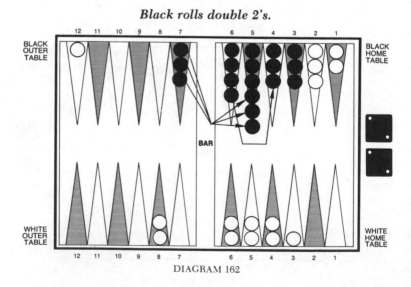

DIAGRAM 162

Bring three men to Black's 5 point from Black's bar and move one man forward 2 from Black's 6 point to Black's 4 point.

148

White rolls 4 and 2.

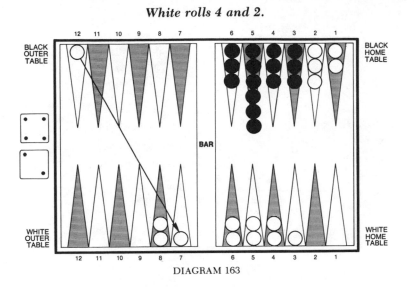

DIAGRAM 163

Move one man from Black's 12 point to White's bar—another builder hoping to make our 3 point or bar point.

Black rolls 6 and 5.

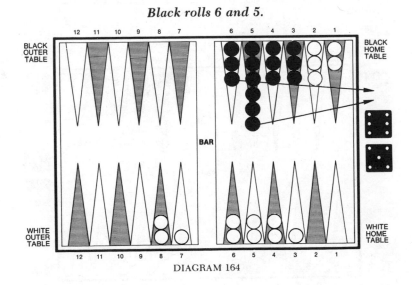

DIAGRAM 164

Bear one man off the 6 point and one man off the 5 point.

White rolls 6 and 3.

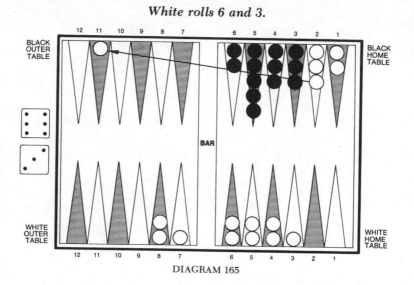

DIAGRAM 165

Move one man from Black's 2 point to Black's 11 point. Only four men—2 points—are necessary to have in Black's board. This extra man will be needed to help White make his board more formidable.

Black rolls 5 and 4.

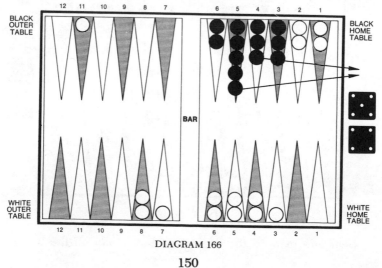

DIAGRAM 166

Bear one man off the 5 point and one man off the 4 point.

White rolls 2 and 1.

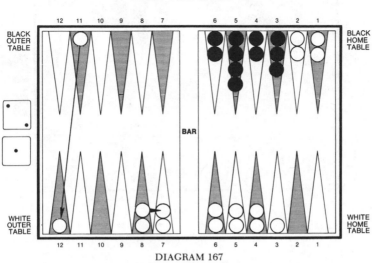

DIAGRAM 167

Move one man 2 from Black's 11 point to White's 12 point and one man from White's 8 point to White's bar.

White's positions will be perfect if we can now make his 3 point.

Black rolls 5 and 1.

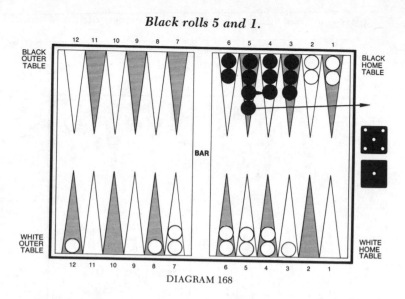

DIAGRAM 168

Bear one man off the 5 point and move one man from the 5 point to the 4 point.

White rolls 5 and 2.

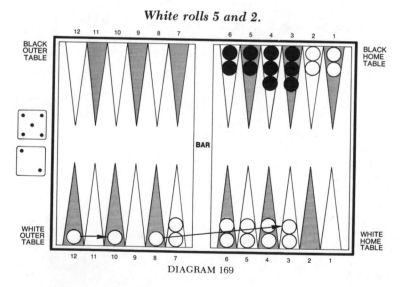

DIAGRAM 169

Perfect! Make White's 3 point and move one man 2 from White's 12 point to White's 10 point.

Black rolls 6 and 4.

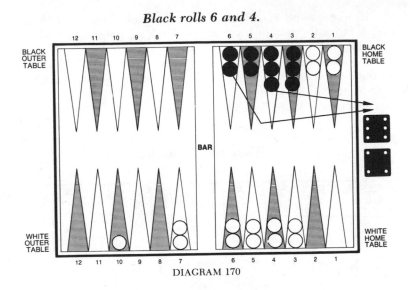

DIAGRAM 170

Things are looking a little better for White. Bear one man off Black's 6 point and one man off Black's 4 point—a forced play.

White rolls double 4's.

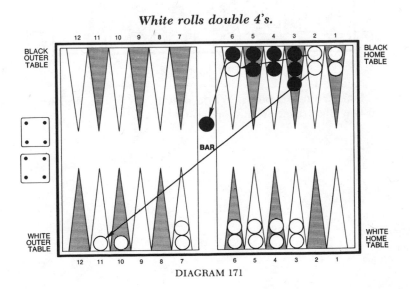

DIAGRAM 171

153

How pleasant! Hit Black's blot on Black's 6 point with the first 4, move the remaining man on Black's 2 point 12 to White's 11 point.

In case Black rolls 2 and 6, which would enter White's board on the 2 point and move out to White's 8 point, White must have men to hit with.

Black rolls 4 and 3 and cannot enter.

White rolls 3 and 2.

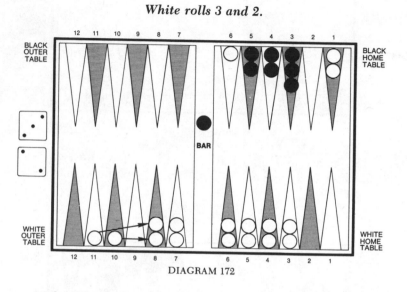

DIAGRAM 172

Make White's 8 point. White now has a prime, and until it is broken Black cannot move past it.

Black rolls 1 and 3.

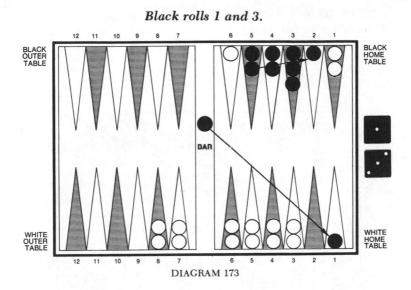

DIAGRAM 173

Enter on White's 1 point, and move one man from Black's 5 point to Black's 2 point. This was a bad roll for Black, but almost inevitable.

White rolls double 6's.

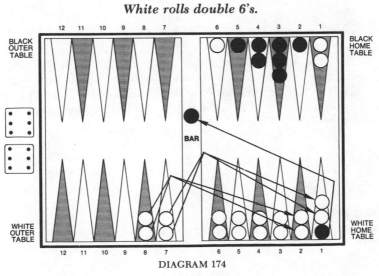

DIAGRAM 174

155

Make White's 2 point and 1 point, closing the board and putting Black's man on the bar.

Black cannot roll.

White rolls 3 and 1.

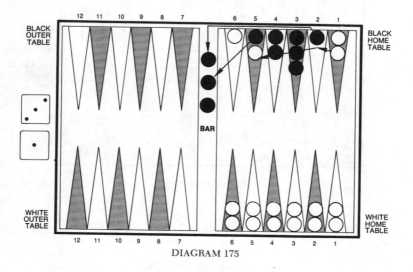

DIAGRAM 175

Move one man 1 and then 3 from Black's 1 point to Black's 5 point, hitting Black's blots.

Since the next few rolls are relatively unimportant until White begins to bear his men off, let's expedite matters by assuming that White brings his three men around the board and enters them as follows: one man on the 6, and one man on the 5, and one man on the 4.

White rolls 6 and 5.

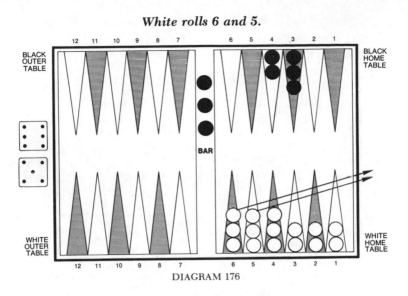

DIAGRAM 176

Bear one man off the 6 and one man off the 5.
Black cannot roll.

White rolls 6 and 2.

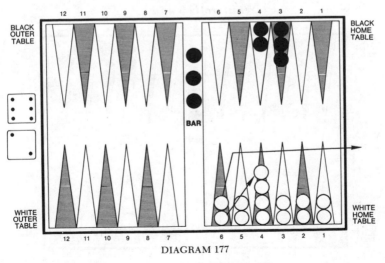

DIAGRAM 177

Bear one man off the 6 and move one man to the 4 point.

157

Black rolls 6 and 3.

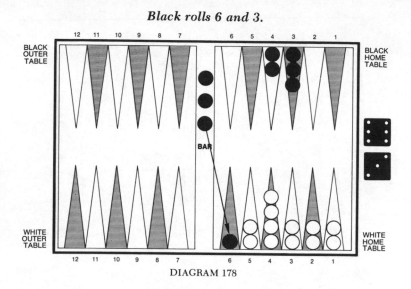

DIAGRAM 178

Enter one man on White's 6 point. (No further moves are possible until the remaining two Black men have entered the board.)

White rolls 5 and 4.

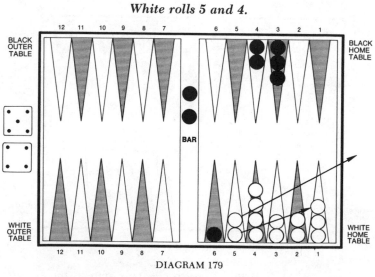

DIAGRAM 179

Bear one man off the 5 point and move one man 4 to the 1 point. White does not want to leave an unnecessary blot for Black to hit.

Black rolls 6 and 5.

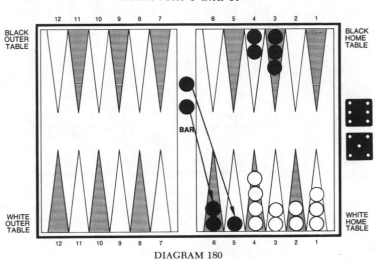

DIAGRAM 180

Enter both men—one on the 6 point and one on the 5 point.

White rolls 6 and 3.

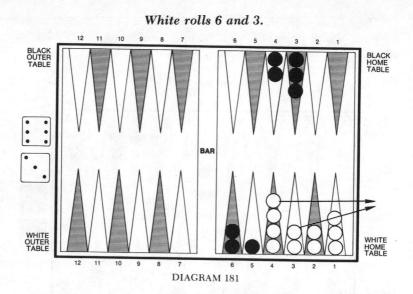

DIAGRAM 181

Bear one man off the 4 point and one man off the 3 point. White no longer has to be concerned with leaving blots. (All of Black's men are past all of his.)

Black rolls 5 and 1.

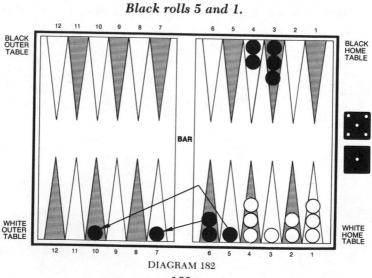

DIAGRAM 182

Move one man 5 from White's 5 point to White's 10 point and one man 1 from White's 6 point to White's bar point. White rolls.

White rolls double 6's.

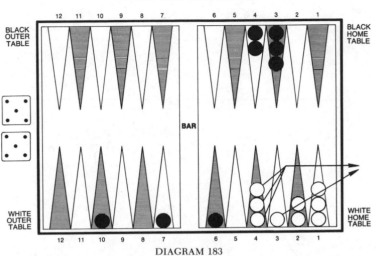

DIAGRAM 183

Bear three men off White's 4 point and one man from White's 3 point.

The remaining rolls are academic since Black can no longer win. Before we play another back game, let's be a little redundant and discuss the prerequisites I mentioned previously:

1) The necessity of being well behind in the running game, a result of your having been hit and sent back and of your opponent's large rolls.

2) The requirement of 2 points in your opponent's home board —preferably the low points.

3) The establishment of the high points in your home board. And remember, concerning the play, that your movement around the board should be slow and your opponent's fast. You must avoid hitting your opponent's blots early in the game, since this will slow him down.

If you understand this—good!

GAME FIVE

White rolls 2 and Black rolls 1.

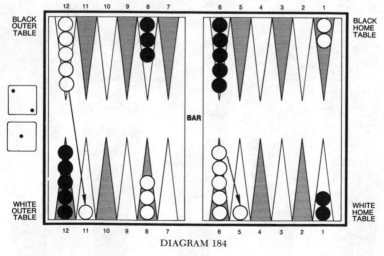

DIAGRAM 184

Move one man from Black's 12 point to White's 11 point and one man from White's 6 point to White's 5 point. If White's blot on the 5 point is not hit, he will almost surely cover this blot his next roll. He has chosen a daring opening move for which he will be amply rewarded if successful.

Black rolls 6 and 4.

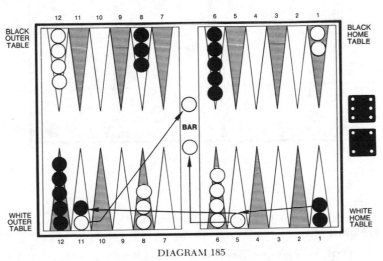

DIAGRAM 185

Move one man 4, and then 6, from White's 1 point to White's 11 point, hitting both of White's blots on the way.

165

White rolls 3 and 1.

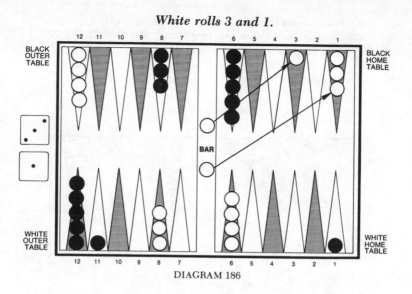

DIAGRAM 186

Enter one man on Black's 3 point and one man on Black's 1 point.

At this point White is too far behind to play a normal game. He must attempt to play a back game. His objective is now clear.

1) Make a second point in Black's board.
2) Slow his forward movement.
3) Avoid hitting Black's men.
4) Prepare his home board and low points in his outer board in anticipation of eventually hitting one or more of Black's men.

166

Black rolls double 4's.

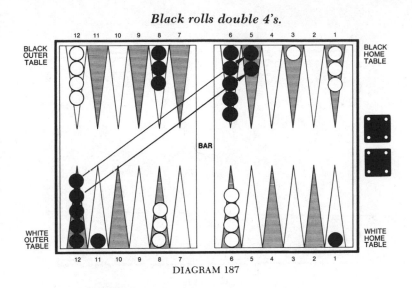

DIAGRAM 187

Make Black's 5 point by moving two men from White's 12 point. Black left his blot on White's 11 point because the establishing of his 5 point far outweighed the cost of this blot being hit. Black also knows that White will make Black's 3 point if White rolls a 2, rather than hitting this blot.

White rolls 2 and 1.

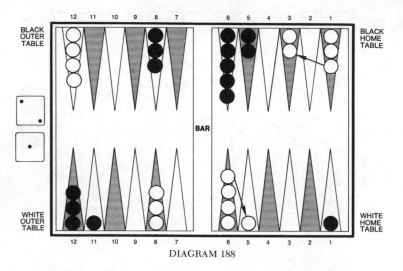

DIAGRAM 188

Make Black's 3 point and drop a blot on White's 5 point from White's 6 point. The second requirement is fulfilled—2 points in Black's home board.

You did not hit Black's blot. That is exactly what you must not do. You no longer care if Black hits your blot on the 5 point, since you have 2 points in his board. As a matter of fact, to slow up even more, you hope Black will be forced to hit another of your blots.

Black rolls 4 and 5.

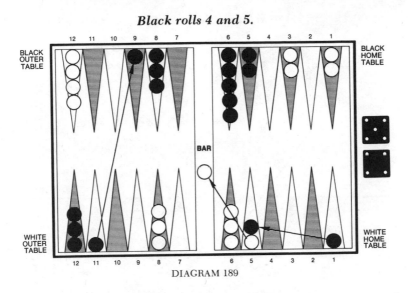

DIAGRAM 189

Move one man 4 from White's 1 point, hitting the blot, and one man 5 from White's 11 point to Black's 9 point.

Black is not worried about being hit. This blot on his 9 point is a builder to help him make the bar or the 4 point.

White rolls 3 and 6.

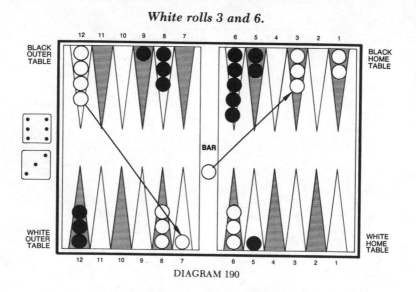

DIAGRAM 190

Enter on Black's 3 point and move one man from Black's 12 point to White's bar. You did not hit Black's blot on his 9 point, for the same reason as before. This would slow Black down, the one thing you must not do!

Black rolls 5 and 4.

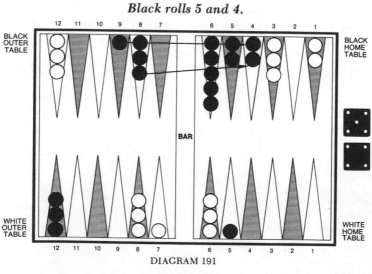

DIAGRAM 191

170

Make Black's 4 point.

White rolls 4 and 1.

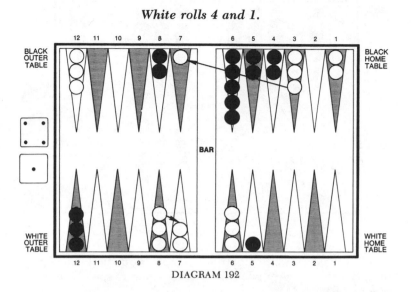

DIAGRAM 192

Make White's bar, and move one man from Black's 3 point to Black's bar. You are preparing your outer board by making your bar point. An alternative play for your 4 might have been to move a man from Black's 12 point to White's 9 point. However, since our game has been slowed up enough already, the risk of losing this extra blot is unnecessary. If you have too many men in Black's home board, you will not have enough men to build your own board.

171

Black rolls double 6's.

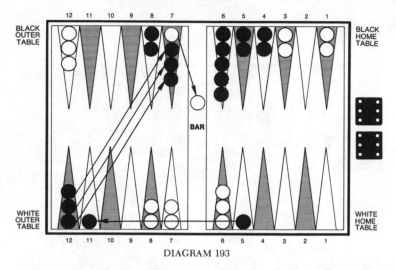

DIAGRAM 193

With what you have learned by now, you should recognize this roll as being very good for White, since it speeds up Black tremendously.

Make Black's bar, with two men, hitting White's blot. Move a third man to Black's bar, and move one man from White's 5 point to White's 11 point.

White rolls 6 and 4.

White cannot enter.

Black rolls 6 and 1.

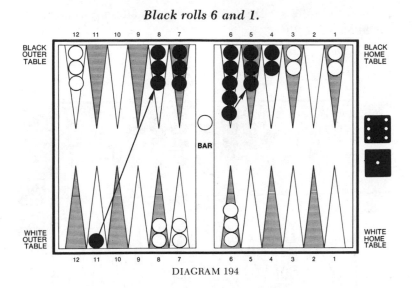

DIAGRAM 194

Move one man from White's 11 point to Black's 8 point and one man from Black's 6 point to Black's 5 point.

White rolls 4 and 3.

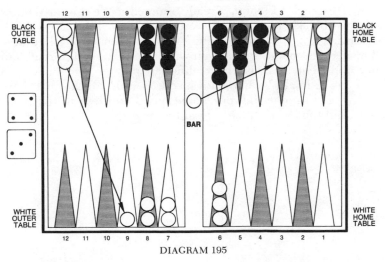

DIAGRAM 195

Enter on Black's 3 point and move one man from Black's

12 point to White's 9 point. You now must attempt to make your
5 point and 4 point.

Black rolls 6 and 5.

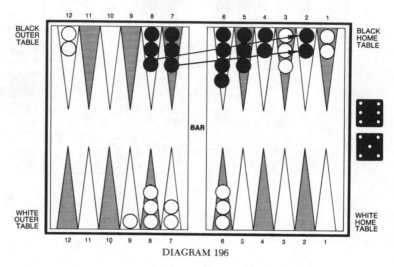

DIAGRAM 196

Make Black's 2 point, already a forced move due to White's
points in Black's home board. Examine the position now. Every
back game you play in the future will look something like this.
Of course, the points which you will have may be different, and
your opponent may also have different points. Your outer and
home board might be more advanced: By this I mean that there
may be more points in your home board and less in the outer
board, but the basic structure will be the same.

White rolls 4 and 3.

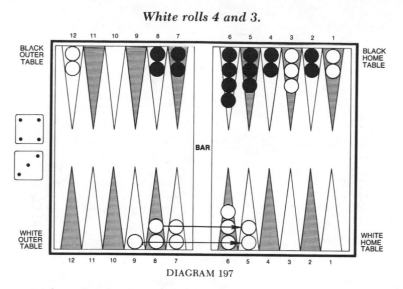

DIAGRAM 197

Make White's 5 point by moving one man 4 from White's 9 point and one man 3 from White's 8 point.

Black rolls 6 and 4.

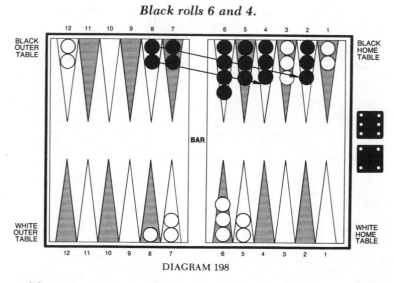

DIAGRAM 198

Move one man to Black's 4 point and one man to Black's 2 point from Black's 8 point.

175

White rolls 6 and 5.

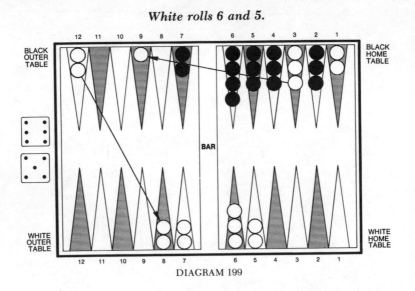

DIAGRAM 199

Move one man from Black's 12 point to White's 8 point and move one man from Black's 3 point to Black's 9 point. Since you cannot make your 4 point the next best thing to do is make your 8 point. You moved one man out of Black's home board, since four men there are sufficient and you can use this extra man to make the necessary points in your outer and home boards.

Black rolls 6 and 5.

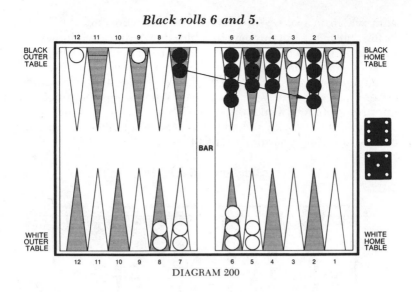

DIAGRAM 200

Move one man from Black's bar to Black's 2 point. Black has no 6 to move—only a 5, and the 5 is forced.

White rolls 5 and 1.

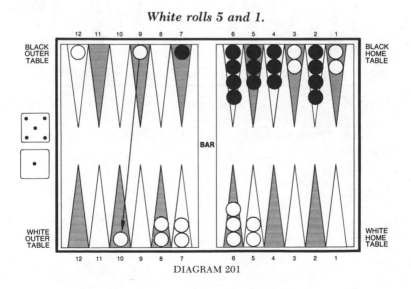

DIAGRAM 201

Move from Black's 9 point to White's 10 point, another man

177

with which to make White's 3 point. You were unfortunate not being able to hit, but this may be a blessing in disguise. Sometimes hitting prematurely can be disastrous. You should not always hit whenever it is possible. There are times when you must wait for another opportunity. You will learn correct timing from experience, but I can help you this much: When your home board is not strong enough (if your opponent's blot can re-enter and escape with little difficulty), you had better wait and hope to get another chance at hitting your opponent's blot.

Black rolls 6 and 3.

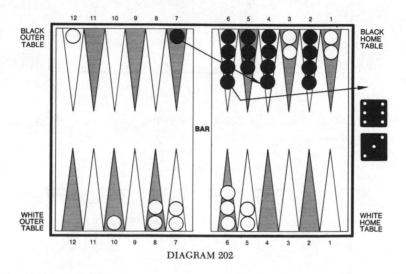

DIAGRAM 202

Move 3 from Black's bar to Black's 4 point and bear one man off the 6 point.

White rolls 6 and 2.

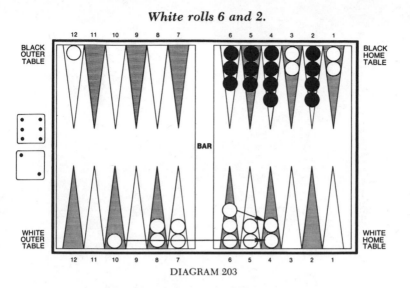

DIAGRAM 203

Make White's 4 point by moving one man 6 from White's 10 point and one man 2 from White's 6 point. You are ready now! If you hit a blot of Black's he will find it very difficult to escape.

Black rolls double 5's.

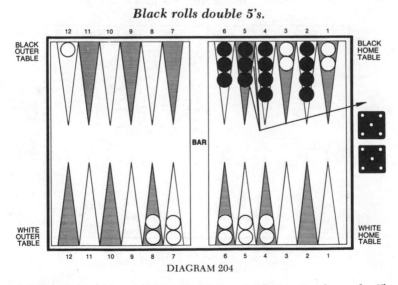

DIAGRAM 204

Bear three men off Black's 5 point. These are the only 5's Black can play.

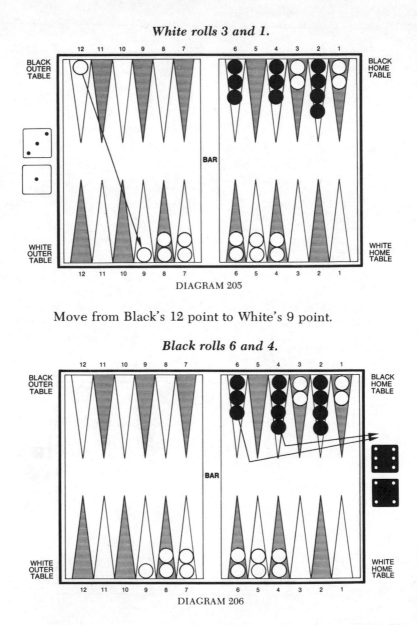

White rolls 3 and 1.

BLACK OUTER TABLE

BLACK HOME TABLE

BAR

WHITE OUTER TABLE

WHITE HOME TABLE

DIAGRAM 205

Move from Black's 12 point to White's 9 point.

Black rolls 6 and 4.

BLACK OUTER TABLE

BLACK HOME TABLE

BAR

WHITE OUTER TABLE

WHITE HOME TABLE

DIAGRAM 206

Bear one man off Black's 6 point and one man off Black's 4 point.

180

White rolls 6 and 5.

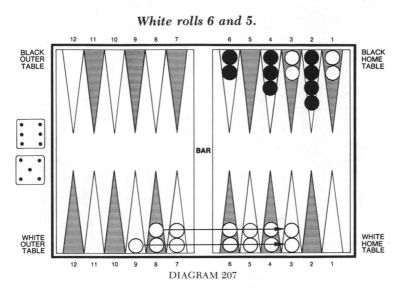

DIAGRAM 207

Make White's 3 point. Move one man 6 from the 9 point
and one man 5 from the 8 point.

Black rolls 6 and 1.

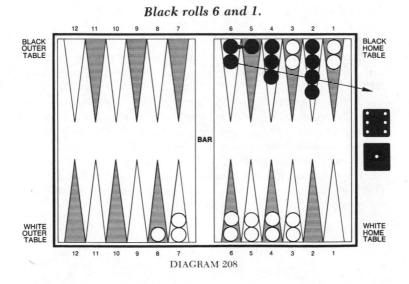

DIAGRAM 208

Bear one man off the 6 point and move one man from the
6 to the 5 point—a forced move.

181

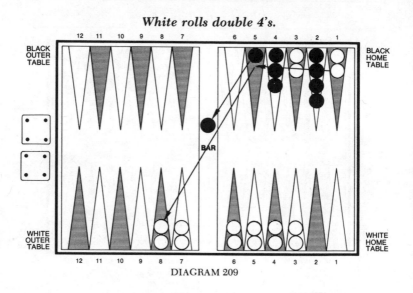

White rolls double 4's.

DIAGRAM 209

Hit Black's blot on the 5 point and continue your same man 12 more (three 4's) to White's 8 point.

You not only hit Black's blot but you made a prime at the same time.

If Black now enters with a 1 and 3 or a 2 and 3, he will be forced to move the 3 from his 4 point to his 1 point. This will hit your blot and give you a chance to pick up a second man of Black's if you enter on Black's 1 point.

It is not necessary to hit a second man of Black's to win this game. A second man, however, would almost insure victory. No one can say exactly what percentage of games White will win from this position. My experience has been that the break-even point occurs when my opponent has borne off eight men (meaning he has seven left), and his remaining men are on the 1 and 2 points. The higher the points that my opponent's men are on, the greater the percentage of games I will win.

Black rolls double 1's.

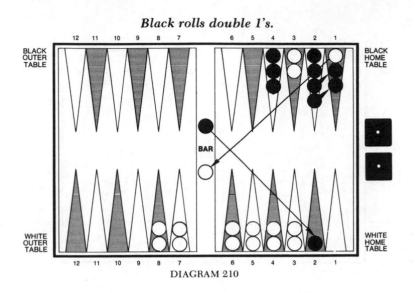

DIAGRAM 210

Enter on White's 1 point and move to White's 2 point. Move two men from Black's 2 point to Black's 1 point, hitting White's blot—a wonderful roll for Black since it decreases his chances of additional exposure. It also makes his bearing off position much better.

White rolls 4 and 1.

White cannot enter. (Don't worry, Black can't go anyplace.)

Black rolls 6 and 5.

No moves. (It's a good thing you have a prime.)

183

White rolls 3 and 4.

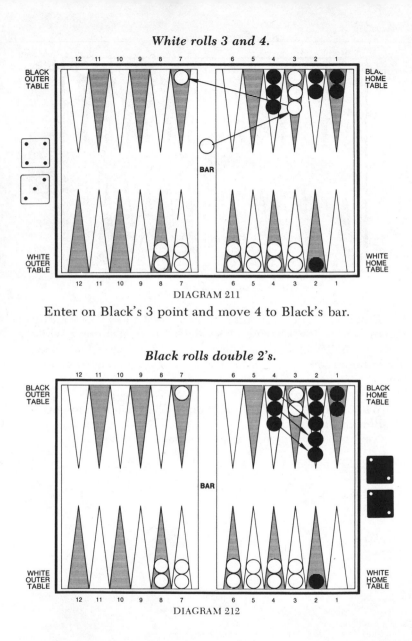

DIAGRAM 211

Enter on Black's 3 point and move 4 to Black's bar.

Black rolls double 2's.

DIAGRAM 212

184

Move three men from Black's 4 point to Black's 2 point—a forced move, and a great one for Black. It is now practically impossible for Black to expose another man.

White rolls 6 and 5.

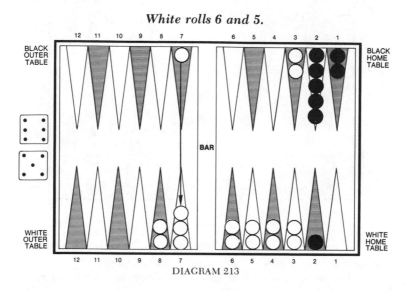

DIAGRAM 213

Move from Black's bar to White's bar. White needs additional builders to make the 2 point. As you can see, White could have made the 2 point but in doing so would have left a blot on White's bar point, which could have been hit if Black rolled a 1 and 6.

Black rolls 5 and 4.

No moves.

White rolls 5 and 2.

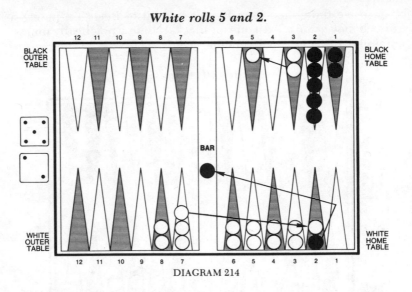

DIAGRAM 214

Move one man 5 from White's bar and hit Black's blot and one man 2 from Black's 3 point to Black's 5 point.

White does not care if he is hit since Black's man cannot escape as long as White maintains his prime.

Black rolls 3 and 5.

Black cannot enter.

White rolls 6 and 2.

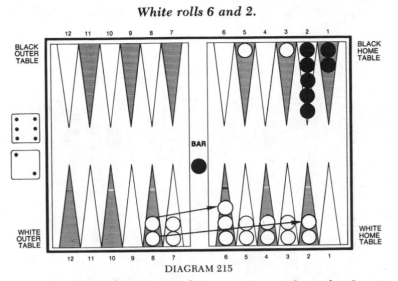

DIAGRAM 215

Make the 2 point by moving one man 6 from the 8 point and move one man 2 from the 8 point to the 6 point. This latter man becomes a builder with which to make the 1 point.

Black rolls 3 and 2.

Black cannot enter.

White rolls 6 and 5.

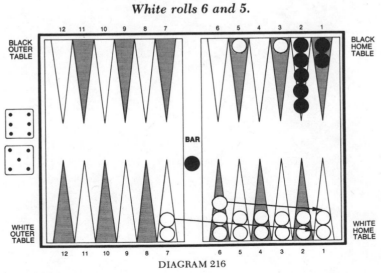

DIAGRAM 216

187

Make White's 1 point. Move one man 6 from the bar and one man 5 from the 6 point.

Black cannot roll.

White rolls double 5's.

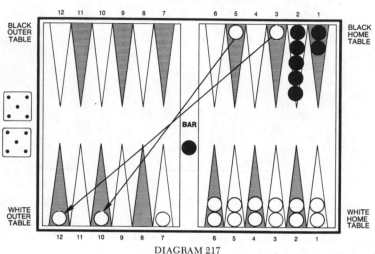

DIAGRAM 217

188

Move one man 10 from Black's 3 point to White's 12 point and one man 10 from Black's 5 point to White's 10 point.
Black cannot roll.

White rolls 6 and 4.

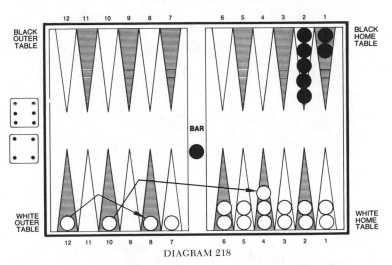

DIAGRAM 218

Move one man 4 from White's 12 point to White's 8 point and one man 6 from White's 10 point to White's 4 point. This play guards against a subsequent roll of double 6's. The way your position is now, a following roll of double 6's will bring the two men from the outer board to the 2 and 1 point and allow you to bear off two men from the 6 point. If you had moved one man 6 from White's 12 point to White's 6 point and one man 4 from White's 10 point to White's 6 point and your next roll was double 6's, you would have been forced to leave a blot on your 6 point. Try it! Errors of this nature are easy to make. You must start training yourself to look for the possibilities of such occurrences. Again it comes back to "anticipating" a certain roll and seeing whether or not you can avoid a disastrous result by moving in a fashion that will obviate this possibility.
Black cannot roll.

White rolls double 2's.

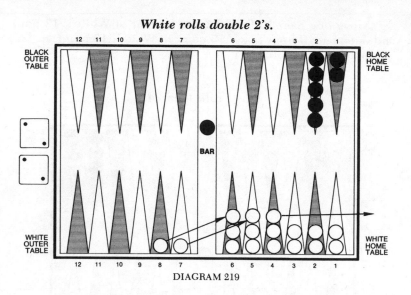

DIAGRAM 219

Move one man from the 8 point to the 6 point, one man from the bar to the 5 point, and bear one man off the 4 point. (You do this by moving forward 2 pips and then off the 2 point.) It would have been possible to bear two men off the 2 point, but this would allow Black to enter on the 2 point and possibly escape. White should attempt to bear off more men before allowing Black to enter.

Black cannot roll.

White rolls 5 and 4.

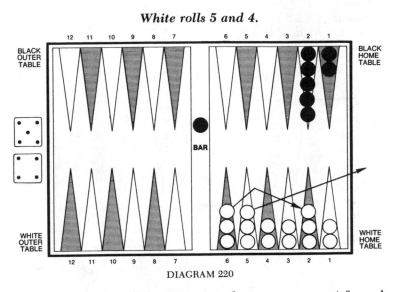

DIAGRAM 220

Bear one man off the 5 point and move one man 4 from the 6 point to the 2 point. *Black cannot roll.*

White rolls 6 and 5.

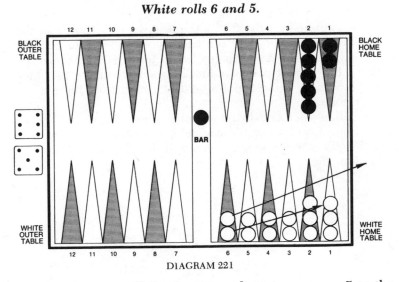

DIAGRAM 221

Bear one man off the 6 point and move one man 5 to the 1 point.

You are forced to open the board.
Black rolls double 5's.
Cannot enter.

White rolls double 3's.

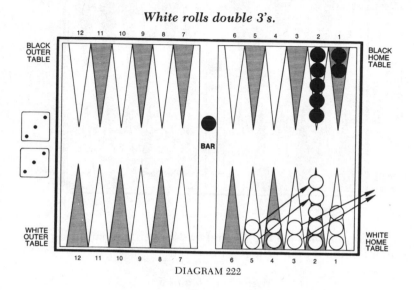

DIAGRAM 222

Bear two men off the 3 point and move two men from the 5 point to the 2 point. If Black had more men left to bear off (he now has eight—seven in his home board plus the man on the bar), the correct play would have been to move two men from the 5 point to the 2 point, and two men from the 4 point to the 1 point.

Deciding whether to bear men off or whether to move forward in your home board is a problem which constantly arises. I can only say that with more experience you will develop an instinct that will guide you.

Black rolls 6 and 2.

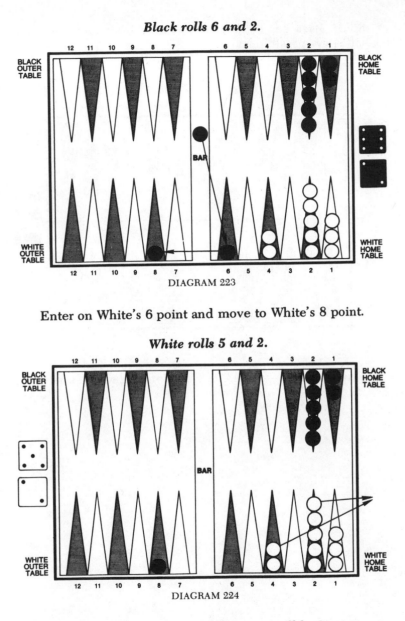

DIAGRAM 223

Enter on White's 6 point and move to White's 8 point.

White rolls 5 and 2.

DIAGRAM 224

Bear one man off the 4 point and one man off the 2 point.

193

Since Black has no way to hit any of your blots, you must take off every possible man.

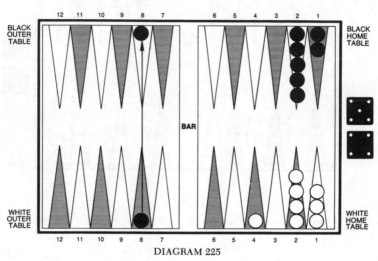

DIAGRAM 225

Move one man from White's 8 point to Black's 8 point.

White rolls 4 and 1.

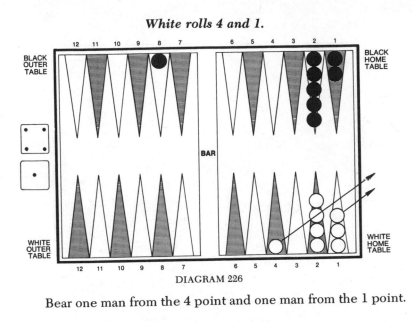

DIAGRAM 226

Bear one man from the 4 point and one man from the 1 point.

Black rolls 5 and 3.

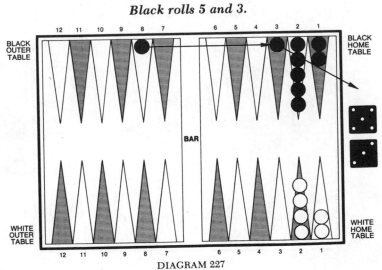

DIAGRAM 227

Move one man 5 from Black's 8 point to Black's 3 point, and then bear this same man off. (The result will be the same as if Black has moved a 3 first and then borne off a 5.)

195

White rolls 3 and 2.

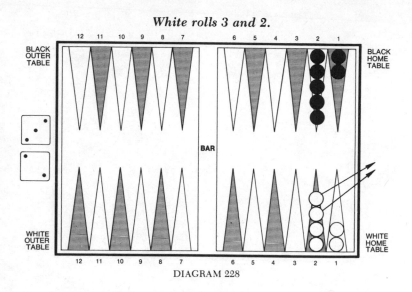

DIAGRAM 228

Bear two men off White's 2 point.

Black rolls 6 and 5.

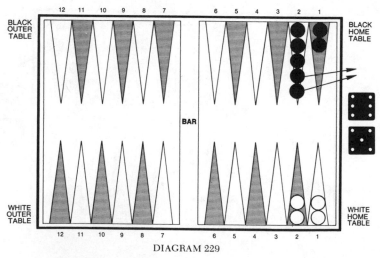

DIAGRAM 229

Bear two men off Black's 2 point.

At this point White has won the game. This conclusion is reached by hypothetically giving White the lowest possible roll (1 and 2) on each of his turns to roll, and Black the highest possible roll (double 6's on his turn).

Since it is White's roll, he must automatically bear off two men with his lowest roll, leaving two men which also must be borne off on his subsequent roll.

The best Black can do on his turn is to bear off four men. This would still leave one man. Therefore, White is the winner.

The Doubling Cube

I hope that you have found the subject of the back game interesting. There are many more intricacies and subtleties that I have not covered. You will discover these for yourselves now that you have a solid understanding of the basic theories of the back game.

The subject that I have saved for last is the doubling cube. Its purpose is that of doubling the stakes of the game when one or the other player feels that he is ahead. The cube or block has the numbers 2, 4, 8, 16, 32, and 64 on its sides. At the start of each game the cube is placed on the bar (or the sides of the board) in the middle, with the number 64 on top. The number 64 represents the number 1, since there is no 1 on the cube. The cube remains in the middle of either the sides of the board or the bar—at "1" until a player doubles. Either player has an option to make the first double. After the first double, only the player who has been doubled can redouble. If this player redoubles, then the cube belongs to the player who doubled the first time, and so on.

For example: The game starts with the cube in the middle

(which means that either player has the right to double) at 1, although 64 will show on the cube.

Let's assume that Black, as a result of some fortuitous rolls, feels that he is ahead and decides to double the stakes. He says, "I double," turns the cube to 2, and places it near his opponent. White now has the option of accepting or declining. If he thinks his chance of winning the game at this point is slim he may decline the double and lose one point (the original stake and the amount showing on the cube before the double). On the other hand he may feel that his chances of winning are still good and accept the double. This means that the game is now being played for twice the amount of the original stake. It also means that Black cannot double again until White redoubles to 4. If the game is played to its conclusion, with no further doubling, the winning side—whether Black or White—will win twice the original stake, unless a gammon or backgammon is involved. If either player were to win a gammon he would win double the amount showing on the cube. If a backgammon were won it would triple the amount on the cube. In this case the amount won would be six.

If White, after having accepted the double to two, were fortunate enough to turn the tide to his favor, he might decide to double back. If White doubles to four, Black, as was White's prerogative before, may accept or decline. If Black's judgment were that he should decline, he would lose 2, the amount showing on the cube before the double. If he were to accept, the same procedure would occur as it did when White accepted the double to 2. There is no limit to the number of times the game may be doubled. The only rule is that if you intend to double you must do so when it is your turn to roll.

In most cases knowing when to double and when to accept will come only as a result of experience, and the ability to remember that yesterday you played and easily won a game that was very similar to the game you are now playing. Don't think that this will be difficult—it won't be. You will be surprised how quickly you absorb general pictures and the outcomes of games you have played. There is no hard and fast rule as to when to double and when to accept. True, there are some positions where you must double or must accept. Once you learn these positions, which you unquestionably will as you play, they will no longer be difficult to recognize. Except for these few occasions, the subject of "doubling and accepting" creates a greater divergence of opinion, among the best of players, than any other phase of backgammon.

If you have absorbed and can apply what you have read, you can say, "I play backgammon."

Since you now possess a good basic grasp of all phases of backgammon, your expertise will increase in direct ratio to the time you devote to playing. Along with your increased ability will be an enchancement of the pleasure you derive from playing the game. The road that I mentioned earlier that an accomplished player must travel has until now been uphill. You have now reached a plateau. From here on your road will be smoother.

A final word of advice: Try to find different people of varying abilities with whom you can play. You will gain something from each. You will learn from those who are more experienced—and you will gain confidence from playing the less experienced. It will also offer the opportunity for you to experiment with your moves and style.

Don't be afraid to ask a good player why he made a certain move. Many of them will enjoy telling you, and you will probably gain some good information. You'll quickly discover those who are reluctant to answer, and won't make the mistake of asking them again. Don't feel that these people are being unpleasant— they've probably devoted a great deal of effort and money to arriving at the level they've reached, and are reluctant to give this hard-earned knowledge away. Perhaps you will fall into this category someday.

Last but not least, always play for a stake that has meaning to you. This stake may vary from ten cents a point to a hundred dollars a point. Play for stakes at which you would like to win—but at which you can afford to lose. Only you can judge that amount.

All right—it's time for you to find your first opponent. You're on your own—good luck!

The Rules of Backgammon

The rules of backgammon have the same purpose as the rules of any other game—they exist to eliminate rather than create arguments.

The following are the official rules of the International Backgammon Association:

1) The game is played by two people.

2) The movement (play) of the men is governed by two dice thrown from a cup.

3) Before the first game either player may ask to roll for choice of seats, men, and dice. Otherwise, they merely sit down, set up the men, and start to play. At the start of a subsequent game either player may ask to mix the dice. In this case that player puts the four dice together in one cup and rolls them out. The opponent selects a die, then the player who rolled, then the opponent, with the roller taking the last one.

THE THROWS

4) For the opening throw each player throws a single die. Each tie requires another opening throw. Whoever throws the higher number wins and for his first move plays the numbers upon both dice. After that each player in turn throws two dice.

5) The dice must be rolled together and come to rest flat (not "cocked") upon the boards at the player's right; otherwise they must be thrown again.

6) There must be a re-throw if a throw is made before an adversary's play is completed or if either player touches a die before it comes to rest.

7) A play is deemed to have been completed when a player moves his men and starts to pick up his dice. If he starts to pick them up before playing all the numbers he can legally play, his opponent has the right to compel him to complete or not to complete his play. A roll by the opponent is an acceptance of the play as made. (See Rule Sixteen.)

THE PLAY

8) The play of the men consists of:

a) moving a man (or men) the exact number of points indicated by the number on each of the two dice thrown;

b) entering a man in the adversary's home board, on a point corresponding to the number on a die thrown;

c) bearing off a man in the player's home board, when no man is left outside that board or on the bar, in accordance with Rule Fourteen.

9) Doubles require four plays of the number on the dice.

10) Plays must be made for both dice if possible. Either number may be played first. If either number thrown may be played, but not both, then the higher number thrown must be played.

11) No play may be made which lands on a point held by two or more of the opponent's men.

12) When a play lands on a point occupied by a single man of the opponent's, such a man is hit and must be lifted from

204

the board and placed on the bar for entry in accordance with Rule Eight.

13) A player having a man on the bar may not play any other man until that man has entered.

14) When in a position to bear off, you may bear off a man from a point corresponding to the number on a die thrown or from the highest occupied point which is lower than the number indicated by a die. If a number is thrown for an unoccupied point, no man below can be borne off, for such number while any man remains on a higher point. You are not required to bear off a man if you are able to move a man forward on the board. Rule Ten applies here in all other situations.

ERRORS

15) If an error has been made in the set-up it must be corrected if either player notices it before the second play of the game has been completed.

16) If an error in play has been made, either player may require its correction before a subsequent throw, but not thereafter.

SCORING

17) A game is won by the player who first bears off all his men.

A gammon (double game) is won if the adversary has not borne off a single man. This doubles the count.

A backgammon (triple game) is won if the adversary has not borne off a single man and has one or more men in the winner's home board or upon the bar. This triples the count.

18) Doubling game. The count is raised:

a) *Automatically:* Each tie in the opening throw doubles the previous count. Automatic doubles are not played unless the players have agreed to use them and an understanding has been reached as to the method and limitation of such doubles.

205

b) *Voluntarily:* Either player may offer the first optional double of the previous count. After that the right to double the previous count alternates, being always with the player who accepted the last double.

A double or redouble may be offered only when it is the player's turn to play and before he has thrown the dice. He shall be deemed to have thrown the dice even if he rolls cocked dice.

A double may be accepted or declined. The refusal of a double terminates the game, and the player refusing loses whatever the count may amount to before the double was offered.

19) Gammons double or triple the last count.

Glossary

BACK GAME—A type of game played when a player finds himself so far behind that neither a running nor blocking game would give him a chance to be victorious.

BAR—The middle strip in the board that separates the inner from the outer table, running in length from one player's side to the other's. In most boards it is a raised partition.

BAR POINT—Each player's seven point—the first point in his outer table, next to the bar.

BEARING OFF—Removing your men from the board, according to the rolls of the dice. You can start bearing off only after all of your men are in your inner or home board. Also called "taking off."

BLOCK—Any point on which two or more of a player's men sit; his opponent is prevented from stopping or landing on such a point.

BLOCKING GAME—A type of game where you attempt to block the movement of your opponent's men by making points.

BLOT—A single man, which is vulnerable to being hit by the opponent.

207

BOARD—1) The entire backgammon table.

2) One of the four sections within the table; each player has an inner or home board, and an outer board—also called inner table and outer table.

BUILDER—Any man which may be used to make an additional point.

CHECKERS—Another word for the thirty men used in playing backgammon.

CLOSED BOARD—Where all six points in a player's home board are occupied by two or more of the player's men.

CUBE—A doubling block with the numbers: 2, 4, 8, 16, 32, and 64 on its sides.

CUP—The vehicle used to throw the dice.

DOUBLE—To increase the game stake to twice its previous size.

DOUBLES or DOUBLETS—The same number thrown on both dice; you then move that number four times.

DOUBLING BLOCK—Same as "cube."

EXPOSED MAN—A blot (single man) which is vulnerable to being hit by the opponent.

GAMMON—When a player wins a game by bearing off all of his men before the loser has been able to bear off any. The winner scores twice the stake.

HIT—Landing on your opponent's blot, sending him off the board to the bar. Also called "to knock off."

HOME BOARD—Same as "inner board"—that section of the board comprising your points from one through six.

INNER BOARD—Same as "home board."

MAKING/ESTABLISHING POINTS—If two or more men are on one point, a player may move more of his own men to that point. However, the opponent may not move onto any point so occupied.

MAN, MEN—The thirty checkers used in playing the game of backgammon.

OFF THE BOARD—Where a man is sent when he is hit or knocked off.

ON THE BAR—The same as "off the board."

OUTER BOARD—A player's bar (7) point through 12 point.

PIPS—A term used in place of points or spaces when discussing movement of men.

POINTS—Each of the long, triangular shapes on the board

are called points. There are twelve of these on each side of the board.

PRIME—Six consecutive or contiguous points, any place on the board, occupied by the same player.

RUNNING GAME—A type of game where you move your men to your home board without attempting to block your opponent.